Igneous Rose

Igneous Rose

Samael Aun Weor

GLORIAN

Igneous Rose
A Glorian Book / 2016

Originally published in Spanish as "Rosa Ignea" (1953).

This Edition © 2016 Glorian Publishing

Print ISBN 978-1-934206-26-3

Glorian Publishing is a non-profit organization delivering to
humanity the teachings of Samael Aun Weor. All proceeds go to
further the distribution of these books. For more information,
visit our website.

gnosticteachings.org

Contents

Illustrations

One of the most ancient symbols in the world, Agni represents the creative
fire at the base of all things, the source and power of the sun, lightning, and
fire. The Rig Veda states that all the gods are centered in Agni (fire).

Introduction

I, Aun Weor, great avatar [messenger] of the new Age of Aquarius, write this ardent book within the voracious fire...

We are now going to enter the igneous womb of the mother goddess of the world.

Agni! Agni! Agni! God of fire, help us, inspire us, and lead us through these igneous labyrinths of great nature.

We are now going to study the delicate petals of the igneous rose of the universe.

We are now going to enter into the most profound caverns of the earth in order to extract its most terrific secrets...

A still, small voice exalts the burning flames of our purest feelings...

The voracity of the children of the fire crackles among the burning embers of the universe...

We feel the crackling of the flames... and the aura of the mother goddess of the world covers us in its purest effort...

Our chalice is of gold, of silver... and it burns like the solemn fire of the universe...

Children of the earth! Hear your instructors, the children of the fire...

Kings and queens of the fire, creatures of the forest... I conjure you!

There is not a jungle without its genie, there is not a tree without its creature, its powers, and its intelligence...

There is not a tree without a soul... Every plant is a physical body of an elemental creature of nature[1]...

Every plant has a soul, and the souls of the plants enclose all the powers of the mother goddess of the world...

---

1   The intelligence or soul of all creatures below the human kingdom, whose physical bodies are the minerals, plants and animals, but whose souls are gnomes, sprites, elves, fairies, etc. (Strictly speaking, even Intellectual Animals remain as elementals until they create the soul; however in common usage the term elementals refers to the creatures of the three lower kingdoms: mineral, plant and animal).

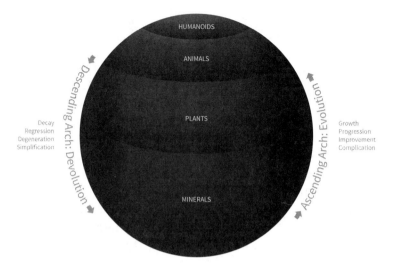

THE KINGDOMS OF MECHANICAL EVOLUTION AND DEVOLUTION

The souls of the plants are the elementals of nature. These innocent creatures have not yet departed from Eden, and for this reason, they have not yet lost their igneous powers...

The elementals of the plants play as innocent children amidst the ineffable melodies of the mother goddess of the world's great Eden.

We delight ourselves with the aromas of the fire. Thus, we arise full of ecstasy towards the ineffable joy of Nirvana.

There is nothing in this ardent creation that is without a soul...

If we observe with the eyes of the spirit the ardent depth of a millenarian rock, then we see that each atom is the physical body of a mineral elemental creature that struggles, loves, and works within the ardent crackling of the universal flames. That elemental intensely longs to climb the ardent steps of carbon and diamond in order to have the joy of entering into the sublime kingdom of the plants...

This book smells of a forest. This book smells of a mountain...

We extract this book from the flames of the universe and each one of its words is written with ardent embers...

We want to now extract all the secrets of ancient wisdom from those giants of the forest, and from those innocent children from the waters, from the air, from the rocks, and from the ardent flames, in order to re-establish the esoteric wisdom over the face of the earth, and to initiate the Age of Maitreya within the crackling flames of our burning powers.

All the elemental magic[2] of the ancient hierophants ardently sparkles into the sacred chalice of the flowers and into the very womb of the august trees of great nature.

It is necessary to search for the ancient wisdom of the hierophants of Egypt and Greece within the millenarian rocks that are challenging time, and within the subterranean caverns of the womb of the Earth, where the burning fire sparks and burns the debris with its flames.

We are going to separate the smoke from the flames. We are going to elaborate the Body of Liberation[3] with the aroma of the most ardent incentive, made from the purest musk.

We need an ardent mind. We need flaming thoughts. We need the Christ mind of the arhat[4] in order to penetrate into the frightful blaze of these universal flames, where the secrets of the igneous rose of nature terrifically sparkle.

We raise our flaming chalice amidst the ardent, sparkling fire of the mother goddess of the world. **Agni!** Illuminate us. We raise our chalice to you.

Let us light a bonfire, and let us sing the ardent hymns of fire within the igneous rose of the universe. Let us raise our august chalice and make a toast to the hierarchies of the flames... **Agni! Agni! Agni!**

2   The word magic is derived from the ancient word "mag" that means priest. Genuine magic is the power of a priest or holy person to help others. "Religion is magic santioned by authority." - Eliphas Levi

3   The perfected body of a highly developed master. In Sanskrit, this body is called Svabhavikakaya. "The Body of Liberation has a Christic appearance. It exudes the aroma of perfection. This body replaces the physical body; it is made of flesh, but it is not the born from the flesh of Adam. This is the body of paradisiacal beings; this body is not submitted to illnesses or death." - Samael Aun Weor, The Major Mysteries

4   "The Christ-mind takes us to the fourth Initiation of Major Mysteries, and confers upon us the degree of "Arhat." ...This task is achieved through the Kundalini of the Mental Body. This is the fourth Kundalini." - Samael Aun Weor, The Zodiacal Course

JUNIPER

Chapter 1

A Queen of the Fire

1. We have now entered a medieval palace. A child plays in this ancient palace.
2. The child climbs on a ladder. We must become children in order to climb the ladder of wisdom.
3. A queen of the fire lives within this ancient palace. She is the elemental queen of the juniper tree, who was incarnated in a physical body in an ancient medieval court.
4. She is a moderate magician. She is an austere magician dressed in a medieval style. This elemental queen has a beautiful, youthful appearance. She lives a very exemplary life in this ancient feudal palace.
5. When submerged in profound internal meditation, we penetrate into a subterranean salon of this ancient mansion. Before our spiritual eyes, a humble bed, a sublime lady, and several holy masters are present. They assist this elemental queen of the juniper tree, who was incarnated in a physical body in the Middle Ages.
6. This strange abode, where one breathes the dust of the centuries, appears illuminated by an old glass spider.
7. Before the bed, a smoldering iron vessel gives off a vague and delicious smoke.
8. The fire intensely burns below this vessel.
9. A liquid boils, and in the liquid is the plant of the juniper tree.
10. The liquid of the vessel is the pure water of life, within which the juniper tree appears.
11. This is the plant of the divine kings. Three Zipas Chibchas of Bacata practiced the worship of the juniper tree.
12. All the divine kings of the past practiced the royal art of the juniper tree.
13. The mantra of the elemental of the juniper tree is **Kem-Lem**.

14. The elemental of the juniper tree resembles a beautiful girl. Each tree has its elemental.

15. All the elementals of the juniper trees obey the elemental queen, who was once incarnated in this ancient medieval palace.

16. The queen begs Agni for help, and this child of fire floats in this strange abode.

17 Thus, the elemental of the juniper tree obeys, and several masters of wisdom appear within the smoke of the vessel.

18. The smoke of the juniper tree forms a gaseous body. This is in order for the invoked angel to dress with it and to become visible and tangible in the physical world.

19. All the divine kings of the past practiced the royal art of the juniper tree in order to speak with the angels.

20. The invoker must drink a glass of juniper tree water during the rite.

21. The chakras enter into activity with the rite of the juniper tree.

22. Each tree has its elemental. The elementals of the juniper tree obey the queen of the fire, who was incarnated during the Middle Ages in a pompous court.

23. The queen of the juniper tree now cultivates her mysteries in a subterranean temple of the earth.

24. When burnt as a perfume, the berries of the juniper tree cleanse the astral body of all types of larvae.

25. The initiate must clothe himself with his priestly vesture in order to officiate in the temple with the elemental of the juniper tree.

26. During the time in which the sacred service of the juniper tree endures, the tree from which the branches and the berries are taken must remain covered with a black cloth and must have several stones hanging from it.

27. During the holy invocation of the elemental of the juniper tree, the initiate must sound a trumpet made from the horn of a ram.

28. The elemental of the juniper tree forms a gaseous body with the smoke that serves as an instrument for the invoked angel.

29. If the invocation is worthy of an answer, the invoked angel will respond to the call. He will make himself visible and tangible in the physical world in order to speak with the one who is calling him.

30. Those who are unworthy can call a thousand times but they will not be heard, because all doors are closed to the unworthy, except the one of repentance.

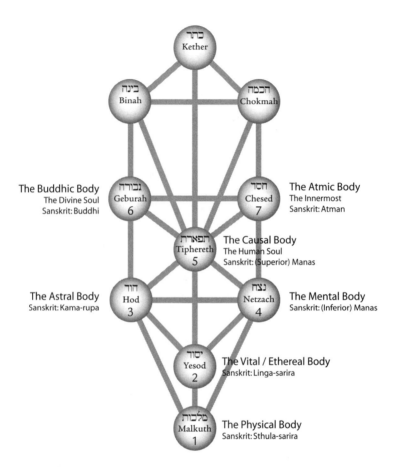

The Buddhic Body
The Divine Soul
Sanskrit: Buddhi

The Atmic Body
The Innermost
Sanskrit: Atman

The Causal Body
The Human Soul
Sanskrit: (Superior) Manas

The Astral Body
Sanskrit: Kama-rupa

The Mental Body
Sanskrit: (Inferior) Manas

The Vital / Ethereal Body
Sanskrit: Linga-sarira

The Physical Body
Sanskrit: Sthula-sarira

כתר
Kether

בינה
Binah

חכמה
Chokmah

גבורה
Geburah
6

חסד
Chesed
7

תפארת
Tiphereth
5

הוד
Hod
3

נצח
Netzach
4

יסוד
Yesod
2

מלכות
Malkuth
1

SEVEN INITIATIONS OF MAJOR MYSTERIES ON THE TREE OF LIFE. TO LEARN MORE, READ THE PERFECT MATRIMONY, THE THREE MOUNTAINS, AND THE REVOLUTION OF BEELZEBUB.

Chapter 2
The Arhat's Seven Candlesticks

1. Hear me, brothers and sisters of the Third Initiation of the Major Mysteries. It is to you that I speak.
2. The hour has arrived in which the seven candlesticks of the mental body must be lit.
3. *"Ere the gold flame can burn with steady light, the lamp must stand well guarded in a spot free from all wind."* – Bhagavad-gita
4. All terrestrial thoughts must fall dead before the doors of the temple.
5. *"The mind that follows the rambling senses makes the soul as helpless as the boat that the wind leads astray upon the waters."* – Bhagavad-gita
6. This is how the precepts of Asian wisdom speak to us.
7. Near to me, oh masters of the Third Initiation of the Major Mysteries. It is to you that I speak.
8. You now need the purest igneous effort.
9. You must now raise your ardent serpent of the mental body.
10. The five-pointed star shines upon the candlesticks of the mind.
11. Within the crackling of the flames, you have now entered into the ardent temple of cosmic mind.
12. Your thoughts are ablaze among the voracity of the flames.
13. This is the igneous temple of the arhat.
14. Your mind must become completely incandescent within the crackling of the fire.
15. There is the need to carefully separate the smoke from the flames.
16. The smoke is darkness. The flames are light.
17. There is the need to practice sexual magic intensely, within the blazing fire.
18. There is the need to convert the material-mind into Christ-mind.

19. There is now the need to steal the fire from the demons of the mental world.
20. Persevere and do not lose heart, sibling of mine.
21. The pedestals of the thrones of the masters are made of monsters.
22. Have faith, my child, and clear your way with the sword.
23. The tenebrous ones are closing the way.
24. Thrust yourself against the tenebrous ones with the ardent edge of your sword. Defeat them and you will enter into the chambers of the holy temple of the arhat.
25. The sun shines and the candlestick of your solar plexus is now lit.
26. Sibling of mine, receive your reward.
27. The solar diamond and the igneous ring sparkle on the ring finger of your mental body.
28. A new igneous rose now burns in your solar plexus.
29. The demons of the mind spy on you everywhere, oh arhat!
30. The serpent of your mental body is now rising through the fine edge of your medulla of the mental body.
31. There is the need to dominate the mind by means of will-power.
32. The mind is the refuge of desire.
33. There is the need to eject the tempting demons from our temple with the terrible whip of willpower.
34. There is the need to liberate the mind from every type of school, religion, sect, political party, concept of mother country, flag, prejudice, desire, and fear.
35. There is the need to liberate the mind from the process of rationalization.
36. There is the need to change the process of rationalization for comprehension.
37. Do not identify yourself with the mind, oh arhat!
38. You are not the mind. You are the Being. You are the Innermost.[5]

---

5   "That part of the Reality (God) within man that the Yogi seeks to attune himself to before attaining cosmic consciousness." - M, The Day-spring of Youth. See glossary.

39. The mind is a wild horse. Tame it with the whip of will-power, so it cannot throw your coach into the abyss.
40. Woe to the coach driver who loses his coach! He must restart his journey.
41. The igneous rose of your heart is your sun of justice.
42. Learn to handle your sword, oh arhat.
43. Learn to separate the smoke from the flames.
44. In everything that is good, there is something evil.
45. In everything that is evil, there is something good.
46. You have now passed beyond good and evil.
47. You now know the goodness of evil and the evilness of good.
48. Offence is hidden within the incense of prayer.
49. Persevere, my child. The serpent of your mind is rising little by little through the medulla of your mental body. The igneous wings, your eternal wings, are open.
50. Your mind shines with the sacred fire.
51. Persevere and do not lose heart. Light your seven eternal candlesticks.
52. Obtain the sight of the eagle and the ardent ear.
53. Your undulating thoughts are flaming within the ardent aura of the universe.

JONAH AND THE PUMPKIN GOURD

Chapter 3
The Pumpkin Gourd
CUCURBITA PEPO

1. Let us now enter the temple, oh arhat, in order to officiate with the pumpkin gourd.
2. Revest yourself with your white mantle and tunic, and approach the altar, oh arhat!
3. We can work with the multitudes with the powers of the elemental of the pumpkin gourd.
4. The elemental of the pumpkin gourd has terrific powers over the multitudes.
5. Jonah made Nineveh repent of its sins with the elemental magic of the pumpkin gourd.
6. The elemental of the pumpkin gourd has a small crown upon its pineal gland that gives it terrific power over the human masses.
7. Learn, oh arhat, to fight against the abominations of humanity by means of the pumpkin gourd. Thus, you will help the human multitudes, and when helping humanity, you help yourself. You know this.
8. Remember that the elemental of the pumpkin gourd has a pink tunic, which is the color of unselfish love. This elemental resembles a beautiful girl dressed with this tunic of love.
9. Jonah was three days in the belly of a fish. On the third day, the fish vomited him onto the square of Nineveh.
10. Jonah then seated himself beneath a pumpkin gourd, and all the people of Nineveh repented. They tore their vestures, covered their bodies with sackcloth and proclaimed a fast.
11. I want you now to understand, oh arhat, the existing intimate relationship between the fish of the sea and the pumpkin gourd.
12. There is a powerful angel who governs the fish of the sea and the elementals of the gourd plants.

13. The current of life that passes through the fish of the sea is the same current that passes through the vegetable family of the pumpkin gourd.
14. The igneous angel who governs the gourd plants is the same ardent flame who governs all the fish of the immense sea.
15. The officiant must place the pumpkin in a pot of water that must boil upon the flames of a small stove.
16. The pumpkin fruit must be cut into pieces before placing it into the pot of water.
17. This pot of water must boil before the altar.
18. The officiant must bless the steaming pot and command the elemental of the pumpkin gourd to work over the multitudes in order to make them repent of their sins.
19. The great White Hierarchy[6] will assist you during the rite.
20. The College of Initiates will collaborate with you in this great work of the Father.
21. The igneous powers of this elemental creature blaze intensely within the ardent sparkling of the universal flames.
22. During this ceremony of elemental magic, the white dove of the Holy Spirit will enter into you, oh arhat!
23. Now, while submerged in profound meditation, you can hear the word of Jehovah.
24. Do not forget, sibling of mine, do not forget, oh arhat, that the spinal vertebrae of the mental body have a corresponding sacred cavern, hidden within the womb of the earth.
25. As long as your igneous serpent is rising through the incandescent medulla of your mental body, you are penetrating into each one of the caverns that correspond to each vertebra.
26. These caverns, illuminated by the fire of your candlestick, burn with splendor.

6   That ancient collection of pure souls who maintain the highest and most sacred of sciences: White Magic or White Tantra. It is called White due to its purity and cleanliness. This "Brotherhood" or "Lodge" includes human beings of the highest order from every race, culture, creed, and religion, and of both sexes.

27. The caverns in which your blazing torch does not yet burn are filled with darkness and smoke. Only you, oh arhat, can dispel this darkness with the sacred fire of your candlestick.
28. The burning fire of cosmic nature sparkles in each one of the thirty-three caverns of the arhat!
29. The sacred mysteries of the fire are cultivated in each one of the thirty-three caverns of the arhat.
30. The light and the fire convert the material-mind into Christ-mind, while the arhat illuminates his caverns with the torch of his candlestick.
31. After Jonah was vomited from the fish, he preached in Nineveh and he sat beneath a pumpkin gourd. He did this in order to work with the powers of the mind that blaze within the sparks of the cosmic mind's glowing embers.
32. People do not understand the symbol of Jonah, despite the fact that Christ resurrected after three days.
33. People ask for signs from Christ, but he gave only the sign of Jonah.
34. Remove your vile vestments because they are filled with worms from all rotting matter.
35. The worm of the rotting matter dries and kills the pumpkin gourd.
36. Only the arhat can officiate during the rite of the pumpkin gourd.
37. The entire Sacred College will go to the temple of the holy rite, dressed with white tunics. Only the few helpers will use light blue tunics and cloaks during the rite.
38. During certain moments, the lights are extinguished and the temple remains in darkness.
39. Now you will understand that the pumpkin plant belongs to the mental plane.
40. Now you will understand all the symbolism of Jonah, the prophet, seated beneath a pumpkin gourd.
41. The moments during the rite in which the lights are extinguished symbolize the passing from the darkness to the light.

42. We must throw out of ourselves all animal-natured, vile deeds.
43. The mantra of the elemental of the pumpkin gourd is "**Ka**."
44. An asian gong must be resounded during this rite.

Chapter 4
The Guardian of the Mind

1. The mind lives reacting against the impacts that come from the exterior world. One must control these reactions of the mind by means of willpower.
2. If one throws a rock into a lake, then one will see crystalline waves extending from the center to the periphery. The waves become the reaction of the water against the rock.
3. If someone insults us, then we feel anger. This anger is a reaction to the words of the insulter.
4. A pornographic image offends our external senses. The mind then reacts as the lake in the given example, with waves of animal passion that extend from the center to the periphery.
5. We must subdue the senses and command the mind with the mighty whip of willpower.
6. Our mind lives reacting against the impacts of the exterior world.
7. The incessant reactions of the mind deliver pleasure and pain to us.
8. Likes and dislikes are nothing more than the result of the reactions of the subjective mind.
9. It is necessary to control these reactions of the subjective mind in order to pass beyond pleasure and pain.
10. We must become serene and indifferent before praise and slander and before triumph and failure.
11. All the tempests of our existence are nothing more than the result of the reactions of the subjective mind before the impacts that come from the exterior world.
12. A clairvoyant examination permits us to comprehend that the reactions of the mind come from a nuclear center.
13. This nuclear center of the subjective mind is the Guardian of the Threshold of the mind.

14. The Guardian of the Threshold of the mind is similar to the smoke of the flame.

15. The Guardian of the Threshold of the mind is a terrible demonic creature. It lives by reacting against the exterior world with waves of pleasure and pain, with waves of likes and dislikes, and with waves of hatred, envy, greed, slander, selfishness, etc.

16. We have created this guardian on our own, with all the evil of our subjective mind.

17. There is the need to carefully separate the smoke from the flames.

18. It is urgent to deprive ourselves of the Guardian of the Threshold of the mind in order to become liberated from our animal past.

19. After opening his igneous wings, the arhat must now pass the ordeal of the Guardian of the Threshold of the mental world.

20. Have courage, oh warrior, oh fighter. This is a supreme moment.

21. Take your igneous sword from its sheath and thrust yourself intrepidly towards the Guardian of the Threshold of the mind.

22. Now you will be free. Now your mind will be under the complete control of the Innermost.

23. When you were longing to be a Chela, you then passed the first ordeal of the Guardian of the Threshold. Now you face the ordeal of the great worldly Guardian of the Threshold.

24. Now you, as a master, have to encounter the Guardian of the mind. Defeat him, and your mind will be free from the external senses.

25. The external wings are opened within the blazing fire of the mind. The tenebrous ones of the world of the mind attack you within the blazing flames. Defeat them, oh arhat!

26. Control your mind with the whip of willpower.

27. When the mind pursues you with perverse representations of hatred or passion, envy or selfishness, etc., speak to the mind as follows:

28. "Mental body, I do not accept this representation. Take it away from me. I do not accept this from you. You must obey me, because I am your lord."

29. The Innermost can control the mind, but only by means of willpower. There is no other way.

30. Let us affirm our Being.

31. "I am not the body. I am not desire. I am not the mind. I am not the willpower. I am not the consciousness. I am not the intelligence.

32. "I am the Innermost.

33. "I will break all the chains of the world. I am the living God. I am the Being. I am life. I am the bread of life. I am the wine."

34. When we affirm the majesty of the Being, the igneous roses of our objective mind glow within the blazing universal fire.

35. When the Guardian of the Threshold of the mind is defeated and flees, the three enigmas of time are broken. Our mind then sparkles with the flames within the great rhythms of the fire.

JESUS WITH THE GRAIL. NOTE HOW THE ARTIST DEPICTED THE GRAIL ACCURATE TO ITS SYMBOLISM
RELATED TO THE BODY, WITH A CENTRAL CHANNEL (THE SPINE) AND THE TWO SIDE CHANNELS
LEADING TO THE BRAIN (THE CUP). PAINTING BY JUAN DE JUANES, MID-LATE 16TH CENTURY

Chapter 5
The Chalice

1. Remember, sibling of mine, that the chalice represents the mind of the human being.
2. The Holy Grail that is in the Temple of Monserrat is filled with the blood of the redeemer of the world.
3. Your chalice is your brain, and your brain is the instrument of your mental body.
4. Sibling of mine, fill your chalice with the blood of the martyr of Calvary so that your mind may be Christified within the ardent sparks of the universal flames.
5. The blood of the lamb is the wine of light of the alchemist. The blood of the lamb is the semen[7].
6. Your semen is the oil of pure gold that rises through your two olive trees to the sacred chalice of your brain, in order to Christify your mind within the blazing fire of the universe.
7. When the chalice is empty, it is the black grail, the grail of the shadow, the grail of the darkness.
8. Sibling of mine, fill your chalice with the blood of the lamb so that it may be converted into the Holy Grail and so that your mind may be Christified.
9. A fornicator or an adulterer can never convert his material-mind into Christ-mind.
10. The masters who are married will Christify themselves by means of sexual magic.
11. The masters who are single will Christify their minds by means of mental transmutation and the sacrifice of sexual abstinence.
12. Thus, the fourth degree of the power of the fire will rise through the medulla of the mental body, converting the material-mind into Christ-mind.
13. You must be pure, pure, pure.

7   In the esoteric tradition of pure sexuality, the word semen refers to the sexual energy of the organism, whether male or female. This is because male and female both carry the "seed" within: in order to create, the two "seeds" must be combined.

14. You are completely forbidden to pour even one drop of your sacred wine.
15. Oh disciple of the rocky path, if you want to Christify your mind, then you must have the vow of eternal chastity.
16. You must fill your sacred chalice with the wine of light so that the fire will make your cosmic mind shine within the august thundering of thought.

Chapter 6
The Apple Tree
MALUS SYLVESTRIS

1. The apple tree symbolizes the sexual force of Eden. When humanity ate of the prohibited fruit, they were cast out of paradise.
2. The angel who governs all the elementals of this tree has the power to close our spinal chambers if we eat of the prohibited fruit.
3. When man violated the laws of the Lord Jehovah, the elemental angel of this tree closed the sacred chambers of our spinal column and cast us out of Eden, where the rivers of the pure waters of life flow with milk and honey.
4. The flaming sword of the elemental angel of the apple tree turns in all directions within the flames that guard the door of paradise.
5. The door of Eden is sex. Eden is sex itself.
6. All the doors are closed to the unworthy, except the door of repentance.
7. Even if a human being would proclaim penitence, if he would fast and cover his body with sackcloth, this alone would not permit him to enter into Eden.
8. Even if a human being were to study all the wisdom of heaven and earth, this alone would not permit him to enter into Eden.
9. Entering into Eden is only possible through one door, the door from which we departed.
10. The human being departed from paradise through the door of sex. Therefore, we can re-enter paradise only through this door.
11. The entire secret is found in the lingam-yoni of the Greek mysteries.
12. The great secrets of the universal fire of life are contained within the union of the phallus and the uterus.
13. There must be a sexual connection, but the semen must not be ejaculated.

14. The refrained desire will transmute the semen into light and fire.
15. The refrained desire will fill our sacred chalice with the sacred wine of light.
16. This is how the sacred chambers are opened. This is how the sacred fire awakens. This is how we open the doors of Eden. This is how we Christify the mind within the igneous rose of the universe.
17. Masters who are single will open their igneous chambers with the terrific force of sacrifice.
18. Sexual abstinence is a tremendous sacrifice.
19. There is a sacred temple in the internal worlds in which the elemental angel who governs this marvelous tree officiates.
20. This temple is illuminated by three eternal lamps.
21. The first lamp is the incarnated rose, which is like the igneous force of the star of the dawn. The second lamp is similar to the blue fire of the Father. The third lamp shines with the immaculate whiteness of perfect chastity.
22. The great melodies of the universal fire resound in the ineffable realm of this temple of Eden.
23. The elemental of this marvelous tree possesses terrific igneous powers.
24. Every plant and every tree has a body, soul, and spirit, just as humans do.
25. Every plant and every tree has its own soul and its own spirit.
26. The souls of the plants are the elementals that play within the igneous rose of the universe.
27. The elemental of the apple tree has igneous powers that sparkle within the aura of the universe.
28. All the brothers and sisters who walk along the rocky path of the blazing flames must learn the elemental magic of this sacred tree, in order to help this painful humanity.
29. We can sow harmony within homes with the elemental powers of this tree.

30. We can perform justice for many unhappy beings with the elemental powers of this tree.

31. A consort abandoned by his or her immoral spouse, a fallen young woman, an unhappy one abused by his or her spouse are cases that can be mended with the elemental powers of this prodigious tree, when the law of karma permits it.

32. Those who believe that they can perform marvels with only the force of the mind are completely mistaken, because everything in nature is dual.

33. To think that all the works of practical magic can be performed with only the force of the mind is as absurd as to think that a man can engender a child without touching a woman.

34. To think that we can perform all types of esoteric works with only the mental force is as ridiculous as to believe that we can write a letter with only a pen and no paper, or to believe that we can have light with only electricity and without the bulb.

35. Everything in this ardent creation is dual. Each thought has a corresponding plant.

36. The elemental of the apple tree is of an extraordinary beauty. It is similar to a bride dressed in white.

37. We can save ourselves from many dangers and mend many broken homes with the elemental of the apple tree.

38. A mat must be placed on the ground beside the apple tree in order to officiate with the elemental.

39. "**Ebnico Abnicar On**" are the mantras of the elemental of the apple tree, as the Lord Jehovah taught me.

40. You must command the elemental with the might of your willpower and with the edge of your sword directed towards the person or persons whom you need to influence.

41. Furthermore, the Lord Jehovah showed me the esotericism of the apple tree.

42. The apple is the incarnated flower that the beast devoured. The apple is the lamb and the beast is the pig of animal passion.

43. And the Lord showed me the apple tree, and behold, the poison of the scorpion within its roots.

44. And the Lord Jehovah showed me a column of white, pure, and immaculate light that was rising towards the heavens upon a plate of embers.

45. The apple tree is the Glorian, and the seven degrees of the power of the fire sparkle around it.

46. And the Lord Jehovah showed me a great mount and many masters of the White Lodge, each one beside his apple tree.

47. And the Lord Jehovah told me, "Only you know what we, the masters, have completed."

48. And the Lord Jehovah showed me an innocent, naked child filled with beauty, and he told me, "This is how we become when we reach the fourth degree of the power of the fire."

49. Then, I understood the teachings of the Lord Jehovah, which are full of wisdom and light.

50. These are the holy teachings of the savior of the world.

51. These are the holy teachings of Jehovah and of the prince messiah, whom we, the Gnostics, love.

52. The arhat is converted into a child. This I learned from the Lord Jehovah.

53. Oh Jehovah! My God! Strengthen me with apples.

54. One day, I, Aun Weor, submerged myself into profound meditation and said to the Lord Jehovah, "Oh Jehovah, help me!" and the Lord Jehovah answered:

55. "I have always helped you. I will always help those who have passed through the schools of the Baalim."

56. The Lord Jehovah wore a triangular crown upon his head. His face was like lightning. His eyes were like torches of ardent fire. His arms and legs were like incandescent metal.

57. Abandon all those schools of the Baalim and seat yourselves beneath your apple tree.

Chapter 7
The Body of Liberation

1. There are two types of flesh: one comes from Adam, and the other does not come from Adam. The flesh that comes from Adam is vulgar and corruptible; the flesh that does not come from Adam is eternal and incorruptible.
2. When the igneous serpent of the mental body reaches a certain canyon, the master then dies and is born in life.
3. The divine Rabbi of Galilee, riding upon a donkey, enters the celestial Jerusalem with the newly liberated human being.
4. The newly liberated human being, also riding upon a donkey, triumphantly and victoriously enters the city where he is received with palms and praises.
5. The master contemplates his body of clay that is crumbling into pieces, and the divine Rabbi of Galilee says to the newly liberated one, "You do not need that now."
6. From this instant, the master is liberated from the wheel of birth and death.
7. A new ultra-sensible physical body, filled with millenarian perfection, has been formed from the finest atoms of the physical body. It has the majestic appearance of the cosmic Christ and is eternal and incorruptible.
8. This vehicle, that replaces the physical body of clay, has been formed in the vital depth of our clay body in the same manner that a chick is formed within the egg.
9. When Franz Hartmann visited the Temple of Bohemia, he found himself with Paracelsus, Joan of Arc, and many other adepts who were living in this sacred monastery with their bodies of flesh and bone.
10. He then dined with the major brothers and sisters in their refectory. Paracelsus instructed him in his laboratory and, in his presence, Paracelsus transmuted lead into gold.

11. Franz Hartmann, in the book entitled *An Adventure in the Mansion of the Rosicrucian Adepts*, tells us these things.

12. When Joan of Arc left her body in the blaze where she was burned alive, she found herself surrounded by masters that took her to the Temple of Bohemia.

13. Since then, she lives in the temple with her ultra-sensible physical body in the presence of all the other major brothers and sisters.

14. This new physical body has the power to make itself visible and tangible in any place and to feed itself with fruits and pure water. The honey from the honey bee is the food of the masters of the universal White Fraternity.

15. When we, the members of the Sacred College of Initiates, are out of this physical body of clay, we function with the body of liberation, which is made from the purest musk.

16. However, when we are incarnated, accomplishing the mission in favor of this painful humanity, we move through places unnoticed just as anyone on the street. We dress in clothes like our fellow men and women. We live and work to earn our daily bread, just as every citizen does.

17. The body of liberation converts us into citizens of Eden.

18. This is how Christ enters us, through the doors of the triumphant and victorious city.

Chapter 8
The Mother Goddess of the World

1. The five-pointed star and the starry cross now shine in the blue heaven of the arhat.
2. Let us now celebrate a feast within the ardent sparks of the universal flames for the Virgin, the blessed Mother Goddess of the world.
3. My Mother shines in her ineffable temple. We must now dress ourselves with our vesture of arhat, in order to celebrate the feast.
4. People believe that nature is something unconscious, but they are wrong. Poor people!
5. When we enter into our internal worlds, we find the mother of all the living beings officiating in her temple.
6. All of immense nature is nothing more than the grandiose body of the queen of heaven.
7. The Mother Goddess of the world is a guru-deva of eternal perfection.
8. We find two altars in the temple of the blessed Mother Goddess of the world, and in the midst of them is the lion of the law.
9. This goddess of the fire has been personified by the virgins of all religions, such as Isis, Mary, Maya, Adonia, Astarte, Insoberta, etc.

10. She is the mother of all living beings.
11. Let us celebrate the feast of the Virgin Mother of the world, oh arhat.
12. The five-pointed star and the starry cross shine in the eternal heavens of the arhat.
13. How beautiful the mother of the world is! Behold her in her ineffable temple, governing all of nature.
14. She wears a brilliant crown of gold upon her head, and her immaculate tunic shines within the sparkling universal flames.
15. Let us celebrate the feast of the Virgin Mother of the world, oh arhat!

Chapter 9
The Cedar
CEDRUS LIBANI

1. The elemental of this tree has marvelously flaming igneous powers.
2. The doors of the cosmic temples are made of cedar wood.
3. The cedar is intimately related with the blazing flames of our spinal column.
4. The devas who govern the elementals of the cedar of the forest have the power to open the incandescent door of our Sushumna channel.
5. This channel is like a small, subterranean passage with its thirty-three blazing chambers of our sacred medulla, where the flames spark within the great crackling of the blazing universal fire.
6. The entrance of this incandescent passage is Innermostly related with the life of the cedars of the forest.
7. We advise our disciples to lie down on a sheet of cedar.
8. The back of our body must be bare in order for the spinal column to be in direct contact with the cedar wood.
9. The elemental of this tree is clothed with a white tunic and a white mantle.
10. The elemental of the cedar has the power to make us invisible before our enemies.
11. The elemental of this tree permits us to prophesy events of the future.
12. The cedars of Lebanon served in order to construct the doors of the temple of Jerusalem.
13. On holy Thursdays and Fridays, the cedars of the forest communicate amongst themselves with mournful sounds that resound in isolated areas of the mountains.
14. The scepter of the patriarchs is made of cedar.
15. When meditating on the cedar, the panorama of future events is revealed before our internal sight. We can then prophesy.

16. When begging the elemental of the cedar to make us invisible, he grants us our petition and thus we remain invisible to the sight of our enemies.

17. The inferior orifice of our spinal medulla is the door of our ardent furnace.

18. The guardian of this door is the angel who governs all the elementals of the cedars.

19. All the doors of the temples are made with the wood of the cedar. "Open thy doors, O Lebanon, that the fire may devour thy cedars." —Zechariah 11:1

20. This is why the door entering into the Sushumna channel is governed by the regent angel of the elementals of the cedars of the forest.

Chapter 10
The Bamboo Reed

1. *"I saw also the height of the house round about: the foundation of the side chambers were a full reed of six great cubits."*
    —Ezekiel 41:8

2. *"And he that talked with me had a golden reed to measure the city, and the gates thereof, and the wall thereof."*
    —Revelation 21:15

3. *"And he brought me thither, and behold, there was a man, whose appearance was like the appearance of brass, with the line of flax in his hand, and a measuring reed; and he stood in the gate."*
    —Ezekiel 40:3

4. The reed is the scepter of the masters of the White Fraternity.

5. The ascent or descent of the sacred fire is registered in the reed.

6. All of the wisdom of the river Euphrates is inside the reed.

7. All of the wisdom of the four rivers of Eden is inside the reed.

8. The reed precisely represents the spinal column.

9. There is a fine medullar channel in the center of our spinal medulla. This fine medullar channel is the Sushumna channel.

10. There is a fine thread in the center of the Sushumna channel that runs along the spinal medulla.

11. The Kundalini ascends through this fine nervous thread, from the coccyx to the middlebrow, following the medullar course.

12. Our spinal column has thirty-three vertebrae. In esotericism, they are known as canyons.

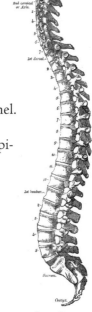

SPINAL COLUMN

13. The thirty-three canyons represent the thirty-three esoteric degrees of esoteric Masonry.
14. The Kundalini is awakened by practicing sexual magic.
15. The Kundalini is the sacred fire.
16. The Kundalini is found enclosed in a membranous cavity
situated in the coccygeal bone.
17. The Kundalini enters into activity with sexual magic. It
breaks the membranous cavity in which it is enclosed
and enters the medullar channel through an orifice or
door that is situated in the inferior part of the medulla.
18. This medullar door remains closed in the common and
current persons.
19. The seminal steam then permits the angel, governor of
the elementals of the cedars, to open this door in order
for our igneous serpent to enter therein...
20. The fire rises slowly, according to the merits of the heart.
21. Each one of our thirty-three sacred chambers represents
determined cosmic powers and a determined addition of
holy values.
22. As long as we practice sexual magic and sanctify ourselves, the governing angel of all the elementals of the
apple tree opens the holy chambers of our spinal column.
23. In the semen there is an angelic atom that governs our
seminal steam.
24. That angelic atom raises the steam of our semen towards
the medullar channel. This is done so that the angel of
the cedars of the forest may utilize it to open the inferi-
or door of the medulla, in order for the divine princess
Kundalini to enter through it.
25. This is why the doors of the Temple of Solomon were
constructed with cedar from Lebanon.
26. In the word Lebanon [Spanish: Libano], we find the
I.A.O. that permits the angel of the cedars of the forest
to open the door of the spinal medulla when we practice
sexual magic.
27. **I.A.O.** is the mantra of sexual magic.

28. The correct way to pronounce this mantra is to vocalize each letter separately, prolonging the sound of each vowel.

29. The mantra I.A.O. must be vocalized during the moments of sexual magic in order to awaken our sacred fire.

30. There are seven nadis or secret centers in our spinal column. They are symbolized by the seven knots of the bamboo reed.

31. Our spinal column truly has the form of a bamboo reed with its seven knots.

32. The rituals of the first, second, and even the third degree, in which we, the Gnostics officiate, belong to the reed.

33. Our spinal column has two orifices, one inferior and one superior.

34. The inferior orifice is the door entering into the medulla, and the superior orifice in the superior part of the cranium is the door departing from the medulla. The terrific force of the hierarchies enters through the orifice in the superior part of the cranium, together with the hiss of the Fohat. It then descends through the profundities of our reed, in order to make the sacred fire rise when we gain a spinal canyon.

35. A door is then opened before us, and a master speaks to us and says, "Enter."

36. And we enter onto a patio and into a temple in order to receive the degree, the symbols and the feast.

37. These are the feasts of the temples and the feasts of the gods.

38. Thus, through this way of ardent and blazing fire, we are entering into each one of our igneous chambers that spark within the fire of the universe.

39. When a human being allows himself to fall, which means, when the human being spills the semen, the angel of the apple tree, governor of all the elementals of the apple trees, is the one who closes the door of one or more chambers of our spinal column. Then, the sacred

fire descends one or more canyons in accordance with the magnitude of the fault.

40. When the sacred fire has penetrated into all of the thirty-three ardent chambers, the high initiation arrives.

41. The Innermost has two souls: one divine, and the other human.

42. In the high initiation, the divine soul is completely fused with the Innermost, and the Innermost is then born in the internal worlds as a new master of the Major Mysteries of the Universal White Fraternity.

43. The seven ardent roses of our spinal column then flame victoriously within the burning aura of the universe.

44. The new master then emerges from within the living profundities of the consciousness. He opens his way through the body of will, and through the mental, astral, and vital bodies, in order to finally express himself through our creative larynx.

45. Now, the master must take out all of his psychical extracts from his inferior vehicles.

46. This work is performed by means of fire.

47. The fire has seven degrees of power.

48. The seven degrees of power of the fire belong to our seven bodies.

49. We have seven sacred serpents, two groups of three, with the sublime coronation of the seventh serpent of ardent fire that unites us with the law and with the Father.

50. These are the seven ladders of knowledge.

51. These are the seven gates of the seven great initiations of Major Mysteries.

52. Only the terror of love and of the law reign through these seven gates.

53. Each one of our seven bodies is an exact duplicate of our physical body.

54. Each one of our seven bodies has its own medulla and semen.

55. Each one of our seven bodies has its own serpent.

56. Thus, we have seven reeds, seven chalices, seven eternal mounts.

57. The medulla of each one of our seven bodies is symbolized by each one of our seven reeds.
58. The sacred wine (semen) resides in each one of our seven chalices.
59. The physical plane, the ethereal plane, the astral plane, the mental plane, the causal plane, the conscious plane (Buddhic) and the plane of the Innermost (Atmic) are the seven eternal mounts.
60. There is the need to raise the seven degrees of the fire.
61. We must convert ourselves into ardent kings upon the majestic summits of the seven eternal mounts.
62. We must grasp each one of our seven reeds.
63. The angel who governs the elemental life of the bamboo also has the power to welcome us into the great mysteries of the fire, or to throw us out of the holy temples.
64. All of our good and evil deeds are registered in our reed.
65. The angel who governs over the bamboo fields reads our book and judges us in accordance with the law.
66. Our spinal column is a great book where all of our past lives have been registered.
67. In our spinal column is where we must learn how to resist all temptations with heroism.
68. Christ, who has tolerated all temptations, is the only one who can give us power and strength in order not to fall into temptation.
69. We must form Christ within ourselves in order to obtain strength, in order not to fall into temptation.
70. There is the need to form Christ within ourselves.
71. When a man and a woman intensely practice sexual magic or when they totally abstain themselves with the terrific sacrifice of abstinence, then Christ is formed within them.
72. The Christ substance extends itself in all the infinite space, and, while we practice sexual magic, it is absorbed by each of our seven bodies until Christ is formed within ourselves.
73. These seven ardent portals are something very personal, very intimate, very individual, and very profound.

74. The path of initiation is something very internal and delicate.

75. In order to possess the reed, the disciple must liberate himself from all types of schools, religions, sects, political parties, concepts of motherland and flags, dogmas, intellectualism, selfishness, hatred, anger, opinions, classroom arguments, authoritarianism, etc.

76. There is a need to search for a guru in order for him to guide us along this internal and delicate way.

77. The guru must be searched for within, in the profundity of the consciousness...

78. Each disciple must search for the master inside, inside, inside.

79. The master is found in the profundity of our consciousness.

80. If you want to search for the master, abandon all bookish erudition and pseudo-spiritual schools.

81. The master appears when the disciple is prepared.

82. The gravest danger for the esotericist is to have a bookish culture.

83. The students of esotericism who have read excessively are commonly filled with terrible pride.

84. The student who is vain due to the intellect feels as though he is the lord of worldly wisdom. He not only lamentably wastes his time going from school to school, but moreover, he closes the door of initiation for himself, and falls into black magic.

85. We must become like children in order to penetrate into the wisdom of the fire, which is deep within ourselves, in the living profundity of our internal consciousness.

86. There is a need to be humble in order to acquire wisdom. Once we have acquired wisdom, we must be even more humble.

87. Esoterically speaking, the seven knotted reed of bamboo is the root of our feet.

88. When we comprehend that the most intimate roots of our existence are hidden within the profundity of our

spinal medulla and our semen, we then understand this symbol of ardent wisdom.

89. Our spiritual feet are placed upon the unknown, and the unknown resides in our reed. Esoterically speaking, this is why the reed is the root of our feet.

90. This symbol is understandable only when we think in the roots of the trees.

91. The tree lives and feeds itself through its roots, and the roots of our existence are found in the spinal medulla and in the semen. This is why the reed is the root of our feet.

92. In a few words, our temple would not have a fundamental foundation if it was not for the reed.

93. The feet of the human being are placed upon life, and life comes from our reed and from our semen.

94. If the human being did not have a spinal column, his feet would be useless because he would not be able to support himself upon them. He would be lacking the reed in order to remain erect in posture.

95. The human being is able to sustain himself upon his feet because of the reed. We now comprehend the symbol of ardent wisdom that affirms that the reed is the root of our feet.

96. Without this root, our feet would not be able to sustain the physical body and they would be useless.

97. All the power of the human being resides in his semen and in his medulla.

98. The feet of the great monarchs of the fire sustained themselves under the majestic power of their reed. This is why the reed is the root of our feet.

99. Woe to the master who loses the power of his reed, because his feet will tumble to the abyss...

100. Each of the elementals of the bamboo reed is an innocent child with a white tunic.

101. One feels amazement when entering the temple of the angel who governs this elemental population of the bamboo.

102. We see these elemental children living a life of paradise in the temple of this angel.
103. The temple is filled with flowers of immaculate beauty, and these innocent children play happily within the gardens of the temple.
104. The angel who governs them educates and instructs them on the wisdom of nature.
105. In this temple of the angel of the bamboo reed, there is only wisdom, music, flowers, and children who play.
106. This is how we, the human beings, were in the past, as elemental children playing in Eden...
107. But, when the human being disobeyed the orders of the Lord Jehovah and surrendered himself to fornication, the fire of his reed went out, and the human being fell into the darkness of the abyss.
108. It was necessary to send a savior for humanity in order to take humanity off the precipice.
109. This savior is Christ. The wisdom of Christ is the wisdom of Melchizedek.
110. This wisdom is found in sex.
111. Eden is sex itself.
112. The door entering into Eden is the same door from which we departed.
113. This door is sex itself.
114. If we departed from Eden due to disobedience, then we return Eden by obeying.
115. If we departed from paradise by eating the forbidden fruit, then we return to paradise by not eating it.
116. Let us again grasp our seven-knotted reed so that we can convert ourselves into omnipotent monarchs of the seven mounts.

Chapter 11

The Prophet Elijah

1. The schools of the Baalim were instituted in the abyss by humanity.
2. The schools of the Baalim consist of all the pseudo-spiritual schools that presently exist in the world.
3. All such external schools are from the abyss. If man wants to leave the abyss, he must liberate his mind from all these cages.
4. When we penetrate into the internal worlds, we find all the students of the schools of Baalim submerged in the profound darkness of black magic.
5. These poor beings are searching outwardly for what they already have inside.
6. All such souls continue to rebel against the commands of the Lord Jehovah, eating the forbidden fruit, of which He said, "You shall not eat."
7. It is painful to see these souls enslaved by the Baalim.
8. The Baalim are the black magicians.
9. All such spiritual schools are filled with fornication and adultery.
10. These spiritualistic schools are the schools of the Baalim.
11. One day, submerged in profound meditation and prayer, I spoke to the Lord Jehovah, "Oh Jehovah, my God. I am alone, fighting against all the schools, against all religions, and against all the sects of the world.
12. "My enemies are as numerous as the sands of the sea, and I am alone against the world. What will the result be in the end?"
13. I then saw in a vision of God the times of the prophet Elijah. One master held a luminous picture between his arms, in which the image of a venerable elder appeared.
14. The elder was the prophet Elijah. His hair was like the unconquered walls of Zion.
15. His aquiline nose and his thin lips indicated a strong force of willpower.

16. His eyes were shining like burning torches, and his white and patriarchal beard glowed with a splendorous, white halo of light.

17. The world in that time was similar to our present time. The schools of the Baalim were as numerous as the present schools. Elijah was alone before all those spiritualistic schools. All the brothers of the darkness looked at him with despise and they desired to kill him.

18. But Elijah was triumphant before the four hundred and fifty prophets of Baal.

19. Then, I, Aun Weor, understood the declaration of this vision. Thus, I attended to the summary of this "matter."

20. I opened the Bible and found what 1 Kings Chapter 18 literally states:

And it came to pass, when Ahab saw Elijah, that Ahab said unto him, Art thou he that troubleth Israel?

And he answered, I have not troubled Israel; but thou and thy father's house, in that ye have forsaken the commandments of the Lord, and thou hast followed Baalim.

Now therefore send, and gather to me all Israel unto Mount Carmel, and the prophets of Baal four hundred and fifty, which eat at Jezebel's table.

So Ahab sent unto all the children of Israel, and gathered the prophets together unto Mount Carmel.

And Elijah came unto all the people, and said, How long halt ye between two opinions? If the Lord be God, follow him: but if Baal, then follow him. And the people answered him not a word.

Then said Elijah unto the people, I, even I only, remain a prophet of the Lord; but Baal's prophets are four hundred and fifty men.

Let them therefore give us two bullocks; and let them choose one bullock for themselves, and cut it in pieces, and lay it on wood, and put no fire under: and I will dress the other bullock, and lay it on wood, and put no fire under.

*And call ye on the name of your gods, and I will call on the
name of the Lord: and the God that answereth by fire, let him be
God. And all the people answered and said, It is well spoken.*

*And Elijah said unto the prophets of Baal, Choose you one
bullock for yourselves, and dress it first; for ye are many;
and call on the name of your gods, but put no fire under.*

*And they took the bullock which was given them, and they dressed
it, and called on the name of Baal from morning even until
noon, saying, O Baal, hear us. But there was no voice, nor any
that answered. And they leaped upon the altar which was made.*

*And it came to pass at noon, that Elijah mocked
them, and said, Cry aloud: for he is a god; either he
is talking, or he is pursuing, or he is in a journey, or
peradventure he sleepeth, and must be awaked.*

*And they cried aloud, and cut themselves after their manner
with knives and lancets, till the blood gushed out upon them.*

*And it came to pass, when midday was past, and they prophesied
until the time of the offering of the evening sacrifice, that here
was neither voice, nor any to answer, nor any that regarded.*

*And Elijah said unto all the people, Come near unto
me. And all the people came near unto him. And he
repaired the altar of the Lord that was broken down.*

*And Elijah took twelve stones, according to the number
of the tribes of the sons of Jacob, unto whom the word
of the Lord came, saying, Israel shall be thy name:*

*And with the stones he built an altar in the name of
the Lord: and he made a trench about the altar, as
great as would contain two measures of seed.*

*And he put the wood in order, and cut the bullock in pieces,
and laid him on the wood, and said, Fill four barrels with
water, and pour it on the burnt sacrifice, and on the wood.*

*And he said, Do it the second time. And they did
it the second time. And he said, Do it the third
time. And they did it the third time.*

*And the water ran round about the altar, and
he filled the trench also with water.*

*And it came to pass at the time of the offering of the evening
sacrifice, that Elijah the prophet came near, and said, Lord
God of Abraham, Isaac, and of Israel, let it be known
this day that thou art God in Israel, and that I am your
servant, and that I have done all these things at thy word.*

*Hear me, O Lord, hear me, that this people
may know that thou art the Lord God, and that
thou hast turned their heart back again.*

*Then the fire of the Lord fell, and consumed the burnt
sacrifice, and the wood, and the stones, and the dust,
and licked up the water that was in the trench.*

*And when all the people saw it, they fell on their faces: and
they said, The Lord, he is the God; the Lord, he is the God.*

*And Elijah said unto them, Take the prophets of Baal; let not one
of them escape. And they took them: And Elijah brought them
down to the brook Kishon, and slew them there.* —1 Kings 18:17-40

Chapter 12

The Pine and the Mind

PINUS SILVESTRIS

1. The pine is the tree of Aquarius. The pine is the tree of the new age. It is the sign of Aquarian thought.
2. The elemental of the pine possesses all the wisdom of the reed. This elemental has an immaculate white aura and is filled with beauty.
3. Each pine has its own elemental because every plant and every tree has body, soul, and spirit like the human being.
4. The igneous powers of the elemental of the pine burn within the blazing flames of the universe.
5. The angel who governs the elemental populations of the pine works with human generation.
6. This angel's responsibility is to deliver the corresponding environment to the human souls in each reincarnation, in accordance with the karmic laws.
7. The elemental of the pine has the power to show future events in the water.
8. The officiant, dressed with his tunic, will ask an innocent child to fix his sight upon a container filled with water.
9. A stone must be placed in the doorway of the temple throughout the entire duration of the rite.
10. The child must be dressed with a white tunic.
11. This rite of the pine must be performed in our subterranean temples or in a cave of the forest.
12. Every child is clairvoyant during the first four years of his life.

PINE TREE

13. If our disciples want to awaken divine clairvoyance they must re-conquer their lost infancy.

14. The atoms of infancy live submerged in our interior universe and it is necessary to self-awaken them towards new activity.

15. When these atoms of infancy emerge from within the profundity of the consciousness, in order to reappear in our objective and secondary system, we then re-conquer our lost infancy and the result is the awakening of divine clairvoyance.

16. We can make these atoms of infancy rise from within the profundity of the consciousness to the exterior surface, by means of the verb.

17. The blessed and venerable Guru Huiracocha spoke to us about the sacred verb of the light through his book *Logos, Mantra, Magic*. He told us that we must begin articulating, little by little, as a child does when he begins to say "Mama."

18. In this book, the Master Huiracocha tells us about the marvelous power of the vowel "**M**." Yet, because this great master wrote in codes, only the initiates understand him.

19. Whosoever wants to re-conquer his lost infancy must again begin vocalizing these infant-like syllables.

20. The words **Ma-ma, Pa-pa**, must be vocalized, stressing the tone on the first syllable of each word and lowering the tone on the second syllable of each word.

21. The mind must assume a completely infant-like attitude during this practice.

22. Thus, divine clairvoyance will awaken in our disciples, with the condition that they must be in the most perfect chastity.

23. During the rite of the pine, the officiant must lie down on the floor while the child observes the surface of the crystalline water.

24. The officiant must then vocalize the syllable "**Au**" several times.

25. A pine branch must be placed hanging above the head of the child. This branch must shade the child's head but it must not touch the child's head.
26. The child will clairvoyantly see the desired place.
27. It is sufficient to order the child to see, and the child will see.
28. The elemental of the pine must be commanded with strength so that he can show to the child the person, place, or situation that we are interested in.
29. The help of the Holy Spirit must also be sought during this ritualistic work of the pine.
30. Our disciples must change the process of reasoning for the beauty of comprehension.
31. The process of reasoning divorces the mind from the Innermost.
32. A mind divorced from the Innermost falls into the abyss of black magic.
33. To reason is a crime of great magnitude against the Innermost.
34. All of the great rationalists are inhabitants of the abyss.
35. Reasoning divides the mind in the battle of antitheses.
36. Antithetical concepts convert the mind into a battle camp.
37. The battle of antithetic concepts causes the mind to be divided, and converts it into a useless instrument.
38. A divided mind is useless as an instrument of the Innermost. When the mind is useless as an instrument of the Innermost, it converts the human into a clumsy and blind being, enslaved by the passions and the sensory perceptions of the exterior world.
39. *"The mind that follows the rambling senses makes the soul as helpless as the boat that the wind leads astray upon the waters."*
   —Bhagavad-gita
40. The great rationalists and intellectuals are precisely the most torpid and passionate beings on Earth.
41. The intellectual loses the meaning of a sentence simply because of the lack of a period or a comma.

42. The intuitive knows how to read what the master does not write and how to listen to what the master does not say.
43. The rationalist is totally enslaved by the exterior senses. His soul is as helpless as the boat that the wind leads astray upon the waters.
44. The process of options divides the mind into a battle of antitheses.
45. A divided mind is a useless instrument.
46. When the mind is a useless instrument for the Innermost, it is then a useful instrument for the animal ego.
47. The spiritual rationalists are the most unhappy beings on Earth.
48. Their minds are completely stuffed with theories and more theories. They suffer horribly when they cannot perform anything based on what they have read.
49. Those poor beings have terrible pride. Thus, they commonly end up separating themselves from their Innermost and convert into Tantric personalities of the abyss.
50. The process of reasoning breaks the delicate membranes of the mental body.
51. Thought must flow silently and serenely with the sweet flow of thinking.
52. Thought must flow integrally without the process of reasoning.
53. There is the need to change the process of reasoning for the quality of discernment.
54. Discernment is direct perception of the truth without the process of reasoning.
55. Discernment is comprehension without the necessity of reasoning.
56. We must change the process of reasoning for the beauty of comprehension.
57. We must liberate the mind from every type of preconception, desire, fear, hatred, school, etc.

58. All of these defects are obstacles that anchor the mind to the external senses.

59. These obstacles convert the mind into a useless instrument for the Innermost.

60. The mind must convert itself into a flexible and delicate instrument through which the Innermost can express Himself.

61. The mind must convert itself into a flame of the universe.

62. The material-mind must convert itself into a Christ-mind.

63. There is the need to control the mind by means of will-power.

64. When the mind aggravates us with useless representations, let us talk to the mind like this, "Mental body, take this representation away from me. You are my slave; I am your lord."

65. Then, like an enchantment, the useless representations that are aggravating us will disappear from our mind.

66. Up to this present moment, the mental body of the human race is found to be in the dawning of its evolution.

67. We corroborate this affirmation by clairvoyantly observing the physiognomy of the mental body of the human beings.

68. The face of the mental body of almost all the human beings has an animal appearance.

69. When we observe all the habits and customs of the human species, we then comprehend why the mental body of most people has an animal physiognomy.

70. The Kundalini of the mental body converts the material-mind into Christ-mind.

71. When the igneous rose of the larynx of the mental body ardently sparks within the universal flames, the arhat then speaks the great verb of light within the august brightness of thought.

72. The mind must become completely infant-like.

73. The mind must convert itself into a child filled with beauty.
74. The pine is the tree of Aquarius.
75. The magic of the pine is entirely related with children.
76. The pine is the Christmas tree.
77. The pine is the tree of the God-Child.
78. We must re-conquer our lost infancy.
79. The pine is the symbol of the mind of the new age.

Chapter 13

The Lord Jehovah

1. When studying Genesis we read that the Lord Jehovah created every herb, every seed, every beast of the earth, every fish of the sea and every living being.
2. This has been read by the majority of human beings. Yet, not all of them have comprehended it.
3. As well, the esotericists have not been able to give us a satisfactory explanation regarding the book of Genesis.
4. The widest variety of interpretations about Jehovah has been given by the esotericists. However, none of them have been able to satisfactory explain who Jehovah is, or how and in what manner He created all the living beings that populate the face of the earth.
5. When we penetrate into the internal worlds, we then comprehend that the Lord Jehovah is a guru-deva. He is the chief of all angelic or devic evolution.
6. Only in this manner can we explain the creation of all things, as told in the book of Genesis.
7. Angels or devas governs all the elementals of the whole of creation. The supreme commander of the angelic or devic evolution governs all the devas, with all the elementals of the whole of creation. This commander is the Lord Jehovah.
8. There is no plant that is without soul. Angels, who in turn are governed by the Lord Jehovah, govern all the souls of plants.
9. The same happens with the mineral and animal elementals. All of them obey the orders of the angels, and every angel obeys the Lord Jehovah.
10. The elementals of the earth, air, water, and fire are incarnated in the plants. Not one seed can sprout without the presence of an elemental.
11. The same happens with animals. Every animal is the physical body of an elemental of nature. All elementals obey the angels. All of the angels work in the great labo-

ratory of nature, under the ardent direction of the Lord Jehovah.

12. The Elohim or Prajapratis of the India of the East are the constructors of this universe.

13. These Elohim work within the blazing flames of the igneous rose of nature, in accordance with the plans of the Lord Jehovah.

14. We now explain to ourselves how and the manner in which the Lord Jehovah created all things in the dawn of life.

15. The Elohim or Prajapratis are the same devas or angels that govern the whole of creation within the crackling, blazing flames of the universe.

16. The students of Heindel remember the Lord Jehovah as an ancient god who had already completed his mission.

17. This false concept of Heindel's students totally collapses when we comprehend that the entire devic evolution works under the direct regency of the Lord Jehovah.

18. There is not one plant that can exist without the presence of an elemental. Every elemental depends on the orders of the angels that work within the igneous rose of the universe, under the orders of the Lord Jehovah.

19. Therefore, the Lord Jehovah creates daily within the blazing flames of this igneous rose of nature.

20. Every master expresses himself through his disciples.

21. The Lord Jehovah expresses himself through his elemental devas, within the eternal instances of life.

22. The Lord Jehovah is a flame that is burning now. We understand this when we understand that our planetary globe is presently preparing itself for the new Aquarian Age.

23. When the master reaches the Fourth Initiation of Major Mysteries, seven paths are opened before him:

24. First: To enter Nirvana.
    Second: To do superior works in Nirvana.
    Third: To form part of the major government of the Logos of the solar system.

Fourth: To remain as a Nirmanakaya, working in the astral plane for humanity.

Fifth: To work in the future Jupiterian period of our earth.

Sixth: To reincarnate in order to work for humanity.

Seventh: To enter the devic or angelic evolution in order to work in this great laboratory of nature under the direct orders of the Lord Jehovah.

25. The Lord Jehovah was not only the creator in the past, but He is also the creator in the present, and He will be the creator in the future.

26. The twelve great zodiacal hierarchies created humanity. However, humanity could not have lived on the physical, chemical earth without the hard work of the Lord Jehovah.

27. From this point of view, the Lord Jehovah created man in his own image and after his own likeness.

28. God created everything with the lost word.

29. The masters that live in Asia have this word very well guarded.

30. A great philosopher once said, "Search for it in China and maybe you will find it in the great Tartar."

31. The lost word is like a gigantic fish, half blue, half green, emerging from the depth of the ocean.

32. Jehovah is the God of the prophets of the past, the present and the future.

33. I, Aun Weor, am a prophet of Jehovah.

THE TOWER OF BABEL

Chapter 14
The Word

1.   *"In the beginning was the Word [Logos], and the Word was with
    God, and the Word was God.*

   "The same was in the beginning with God.

   *"All things were made by him; and without him
   was not any thing made that was made.*

   "In him was life; and the life was the light of men.

   *"And the light shineth in the darkness; and
   the darkness comprehended it not.*

   "There was a man sent from God, whose name was John.

   *"The same came for a witness, to bear witness of the
   Light, that all men through him might believe.*

   "He was not that Light, but sent to bear witness of that Light.

   *"That was the true Light, which lighteth every
   man that cometh into the world.*

   *"He was in the world, and the world was made
   by him, and the world knew him not.*

   "He came into his own, and his own received him not.

   *"But as many as received him, to them gave he power to
   become sons of God, even to them that believe on his name:*

   *"Which were born, not of blood, nor of the will of
   the flesh, nor of the will of man, but of God.*

   *"And the Word was made flesh, and dwelt among us,
   and we beheld his glory, the glory as of the only begotten
   of the Father, full of grace and truth."* —John 1:1-14

2.   The Word is deposited in the semen.

3. The luminous and spermatic FIAT of the first instant sleeps at the bottom of our holy ark, awaiting the moment to be realized.
4. The entire universe is the incarnation of the Word.
5. This Word is the Christonic substance of the Solar Logos.
6. In ancient times, mankind spoke the divine solar language, and all the creatures of the earth, water, air, and fire knelt before mankind in obedience.
7. But, when mankind ate of the forbidden fruit, he forgot the language of the children of the fire, and built the Tower of Babel.
8. This tower symbolizes all the languages of the world.
9. Consequently, human beings were left confused amongst themselves with many languages.
10. In ancient times, only the language of Eden was spoken. The children of the fire created all things with this sacred Word.
11. And the Word came into this world, and the Word was hung upon a beam in the majestic summits of Calvary. *"He came into his own, and his own received him not."*
12. The Word *"is the true light which lights every human who comes into the world."*
13. When the sacred serpent reaches our larynx, we then acquire the power to speak the divine language that we possessed in the Age of the Titans, when the rivers flowed with milk and honey.
14. Then, we were giants.
15. In order to speak the golden Word, there is the need to practice sexual magic intensely, because the Word of the Solar Logos abides in our Christonic semen.
16. Your mind shines with the sacred fire, oh arhat!
17. Your mind flames within the undulating flames of space.
18. The igneous roses of your mental body ardently spark within the glowing embers of your mind.
19. A new igneous rose now shines ardently in your mind. It is the igneous rose of the throat of your mental body.

20. The chalice shines upon the tree of your existence. The sun glows within the ardent space...

21. Now enter, oh arhat, into the holy temple of the cosmic mind, so that you may receive the symbol and the solemn feast of the Word that resounds in the whole of creation within the ardent rhythms of the Mahavan and the Chotavan.

22. The flames of space ardently hiss within the igneous rose of your throat.

23. Remember, my child, that all things of the universe are nothing but the granules of the Fohat.[8]

24. Listen to me, my child:

25. Now, your throat is the living incarnation of the Word of the gods.

26. Listen to me, oh arhat, the flames of the universe now speak through your creative larynx, unleashing tempests upon the multitudes.

27. Jerusalem! Jerusalem! The beloved city of the prophets. *How often would I have gathered your children together, just as a hen gathers her chickens under her wings, and you did not want it!* [Matthew 23:37, Luke 13:34]

28. The Word of the sacred flames was expressed through the ardent larynx of the prophets of Zion. The unconquered walls of the beloved city of the prophets collapsed before the omnipotent power of the Word.

29. When speaking the Word of light, the blazing flames of the cosmic mind are terribly divine.

30. Your mind is now a blazing fire, oh arhat!

31. Your fourth serpent has now converted you into an ardent dragon of the Word.

32. The sexual force of Eden has now flourished in "your fertile lips, made Word."

---

8   A term used by H.P. Blavatsky to represent the active (male) potency of the Shakti (female sexual power) in nature, the essence of cosmic electricity, vital force.

THE POMEGRANATE TREE (PINUCA GRANATUM)

"With the elemental magic of
the pomegranate, you can work
for the progress of peace."

Chapter 15

Magic of the Pomegranate Tree, Orange Tree, Spikenard, Saffron, Cinnamon, Frankincense, Myrrh, Aloe, Storax Tree, Mint, and Fig Tree

The Pomegranate Tree
PINUCA GRANATUM

1. The pomegranate tree represents friendship.
2. The pomegranate tree represents friendly agreements.
3. The pomegranate tree represents home.
4. The elementals of the pomegranate trees have the power to establish friendly relationships.
5. The elementals of the pomegranate trees have the power to establish fraternal agreements among humans.
6. The elementals of the pomegranate trees have the power to establish harmony within homes.
7. In the astral light, the pomegranate tree is symbolized by the horse.
8. The horse is always the symbol of friendship.
9. In homes, the angel who governs the elemental population of the pomegranate trees is as the sun.
10. If you wish to sow harmony in homes filled with affliction, then you must utilize the elemental magic of the pomegranate tree.
11. If you need to establish friendly relationships with certain people, then you must utilize the elemental magic of the pomegranate tree.
12. If you need to reach an important agreement with another person, then you must utilize the igneous powers of the elementals of the pomegranate trees.

13. We can work on lost souls in order to help them return to the path of light by means of the elemental magic of the pomegranate tree.
14. We can help the prodigal son return to his home by means of the elemental magic of the pomegranate trees.
15. When the elemental of the orange tree submits us to "ordeals," we can triumph with the elemental magic of the pomegranate trees.
16. The Lord Jehovah showed me a great mount. The Lord Jehovah was upon this great mount, and the Lord Jehovah told me:
17. "With the elemental magic of the pomegranate, you can work for the progress of peace."
18. The Lord Jehovah had the figure of the white dove of the Holy Spirit.
19. The entire great mount shone, filled with majesty.
20. With the elemental power of the pomegranates we can work on fornicators in order to help them to depart from the abyss.
21. We stated that we can defend ourselves with the elemental magic of the pomegranate tree, when the elemental genii of the orange trees submits us to ordeals. We want to affirm with this statement that the hierarchical currents that pass through the orange trees are the opposite pole of the cosmic currents that pass through the elemental department of the pomegranate trees.
22. Force and forces are something very united in creation.
23. The life that passes through plants also passes through minerals, animals, and human species.
24. In this meaning, the distinct elemental departments of nature are found related with the various states or areas of human activity.
25. Immense powers and innumerable hierarchies work under the direction of the angels who are regents of various elemental departments of nature.
26. Thus, the Lord Jehovah showed me the Tree of Life.
27. This is one of the two trees of Eden.
28. Then I understood the teachings of Jehovah.

29. When we work for the progress of peace, for the universal fraternity, for the dignity of homes, we are using the elemental magic of the pomegranates.
30. This means that we are intensely living with the elemental magic of the pomegranate in those moments.
31. The glory of the Lord Jehovah shines upon the mount of peace.
32. **Vago O A Ego**. These are the mantras of the elementals of the pomegranates.
33. When we wish to utilize the elemental of the pomegranate tree, we must walk around the tree in a circle. We must bless the tree, then pronounce the mantras and command the elemental to work on the person or persons who we are interested in, according to our desired goals.
34. The angel who watches over all the homes of the earth belongs to the elemental kingdom of the pomegranates.
35. Each human family is protected by a familial angel.
36. These familial angels belong to the elemental department of the pomegranate. The Masons ignore the esoteric significance of the pomegranate.

Elemental Department of the Orange Trees
CITRUS AURANTIUM

37. The hierarchies that govern the elemental department of the orange trees are the same that govern the economic and monetary movements of the human species.
38. All the economic problems of the world are resolved with the terrific force of love, which is found in the elemental magic of the pomegranate trees.
39. All disagreements among humans are resolved with love, which is found in the elemental force of the pomegranate trees.
40. All hatred and selfishness disappear with love, which is found in the elemental magic of the pomegranate trees.

41. This is why we have stated that when the creatures of the orange trees submit us to ordeals, we can triumph with the elemental magic of the pomegranate trees.
42. The orange trees are intimately related with currency, and currency engenders many types of conflict.
43. The elemental population of the orange trees are found to be intimately related with the economic problems of humanity.
44. The elemental population of the orange trees are governed by the devas who distribute the seeds of all that exist.
45. These elemental devas also govern the seed of the human species and the seed of the animal species.
46. The devotees of the wisdom of the fire will now understand why the elemental hierarchies of the orange trees have the power to distribute the economy of the world.
47. These devas work in accordance with the laws of karma.
48. Before money existed upon the earth, these devas governed the world's economy. When money stops existing, they will continue, as always, to distribute the world's economy, in accordance with the law of karma.
49. In these times, money serves as a karmic instrument, in order to reward or punish humans.
50. When we penetrate into the temple of the angel that governs the elemental population of the orange trees, we then see these elemental children dressed with tunics of diverse colors.
51. These children study their sacred books. They are instructed and taught by the angel who governs them.
52. The mantra of the elementals of the orange trees is: "**A Kumo**."

Elemental Magic of the Spikenard
NARDOSTACHYS JATAMANSI DC.

53. *"While the king sitteth at his table, my spikenard sendeth forth the smell thereof."* —Song of Solomon 1:12
54. The spikenard is the most sublime perfume of love.

55. The spikenard is the perfume of those who have crossed to the other shore.
56. The spikenard belongs to the human soul (causal body or body of willpower, superior manas).
57. The spikenard is the perfume of the Fifth Initiation of Major Mysteries.
58. The spikenard belongs to the Christified causal body.
59. The spikenard is the perfume of the higher initiates.
60. The spikenard is a plant that belongs to the causal plane.
61. The spikenard is the perfume of liberation.
62. The spikenard is the perfume of the hierophants of Major Mysteries.
63. Esoterically speaking, we must lead great battles in order to obtain the spikenard.
64. The perfume of the spikenard efficiently acts on the consciousness of artists.
65. Wherever art and beauty are present, the fragrance of the spikenard must also be present.
66. The planet of the spikenard is Saturn.
67. The mantra of the elemental population of the spikenard is "**Atoya**."
68. The elemental creatures of the spikenards can be utilized for goals of friendship.
69. The spikenard is the perfume of the new Aquarian Age.

Elemental Magic of the Saffron
CROCUS SAVITUS

70. The saffron is the plant of the apostolate.
71. The elemental population of the saffron is found to be intimately related with the apostolate.
72. The apostle is a martyr of the cosmic mind.
73. The mind of the authentic apostle is crucified.
74. The mind of the authentic apostle is intimately related with the elemental department of the saffron.
75. The mind of the arhat is intimately related with this elemental department of the saffron.
76. The apostle is a martyr.

77. Everyone in the world benefits from the works of the apostles. Everyone in the world reads their books. Everyone in the world pays the apostle with the coin of ingratitude because, according to popular concept, "the apostle has not the right to know."
78. However, all the great works of the world are due to the apostles.
79. The saffron is intimately related with the great apostles of art: Beethoven, Mozart, Berlioz, Wagner, Bach, etc.
80. The planet related to saffron is Venus, the star of love.
81. Every apostle is intimately related with the elemental magic of the saffron.
82. The apostle hangs from a very bitter rope, and below him lies a deep abyss.
83. The elemental department of the saffron is intimately related with hard work.
84. The work of an apostle of the light, the work of the one who fights for his daily bread, and the hard work of the minute bees is immensely sacred and intimately related with this elemental department of the saffron.
85. Not one form of honest work, no matter how simple it may be, can ever be despised, because work in all its forms is intimately related with the cosmic hierarchies who are related with this elemental department of the saffron.
86. Every detail, every circumstance of work, as insignificant as it may appear, invests gigantic proportions within the activity of evolving life.
87. An insignificant bee that falls and is wounded far from its hive is an event, a moral tragedy, a frightful drama for all the bees of the hive.
88. This event can only be compared with something similar related with the human species.
89. A human family is filled with profound desperation when a son, a brother, or the head of the family cannot return home, because they have been injured at work, or because they have been hit by a car in the street, or because of any similar accident.

90. All of his relatives, desperate with pain, will try to resolve the situation so that he is able to return home.

91. The same tragedy, the same painful drama, happens with the insignificant bee.

92. The bee is small in comparison to ourselves, we see it as being tiny. But the bees amongst themselves see each other in the same form as one person sees another person. They do not see themselves as being tiny, nor do they feel small.

93. The mind of the arhat must deeply comprehend all of these intimate activities related with the elemental department of the saffron.

94. In every type of work, as minute as it may be, there is happiness and there is sadness. There are profound moral tragedies that invite us to comprehend the sublime greatness of any type of work performed by the human species, by the insignificant insect and as well, by the apostle who works for the benefit of humanity.

95. The elementals of the saffron have beautiful tunics of a pale pink color.

96. The saffron and the bee are a symbol of work, and both are governed by the planet Venus.

Elemental Magic of the Cinnamon
CINNAMOMUM CEYLANICUM

97. Cinnamon is related to cordiality, and is a restorative of forces.

98. Wherever there is happiness the elemental magic of the cinnamon surely must be present.

99. Wherever there is activity and optimism, the elemental magic of the cinnamon is present.

100. The elemental magic of the cinnamon gives activity and happiness.

101. Optimism and happiness must be combined with all our activities.

102. The elemental department of the cinnamon is precisely related with optimism and happiness.

103. The elemental magic of the cinnamon is intimately related with elemental forces that restore and comfort our life.

104. The elemental magic of the cinnamon is found intimately related with the forces that restore, fortify and comfort the life of children, adolescents, women, and elders.

105. The mind of the arhat must cultivate optimism and happiness.

106. Wherever there is activity, a healthy happiness is needed.

107. The mind of the arhat must deeply comprehend the significance of happiness and optimism.

108. When we penetrate into the elemental temple of this vegetable department of nature, we see the elemental children of these trees playing happily within the temple, under the watch of the angel who directs them.

109. We must comprehend the significance of music, happiness, and optimism.

110. One remains in ecstasy when listening to *The Magic Flute* of Mozart, which reminds us of an Egyptian initiation.

111. One feels amazed when listening to the nine symphonies of Beethoven, or the ineffable melodies of Chopin and Liszt.

112. The ineffable music of the great classics comes from the exquisite regions of Nirvana where only happiness that is beyond love reigns...

113. All the great children of the fire distill the perfume of happiness and the exquisite fragrance of music and joy.

114. The elementals of these trees are beautiful children, dressed with tunics of a pale pink color.

Elemental Magic of Frankincense
BOSWELLIA

115. Authentic frankincense is obtained from the olibanum tree. It contains great elemental powers.

116. If frankincense is soaked in water, it has the power to make the elemental creatures of the water concur to our call.

117. When frankincense is applied to the forehead, it has the power to make a headache caused by strong mental preoccupation to disappear.

118. The smoke of frankincense has the power to make the masters and angels of the invisible world attend.

119. Frankincense prepares the environment for the Gnostic rituals.

120. Frankincense is a great vehicle for spiritual waves of pure devotion. It helps the mystical retreat because it serves as an instrument of devotion.

121. In the ancient temples of the mysteries, those who were ill were surrounded with the smoke of frankincense in order to be cured.

122. The creatures of the water happily concur when we soak frankincense in a vessel of water.

123. Frankincense must be burned when we are going to sign a friendly pact. The Aztec magicians smoked tobacco when they signed a pact with the Spaniards.

124. They did this with the objective of preparing the atmosphere for the signing of the pact and in order to have friendly conversation.

125. However, we recommend the burning of frankincense for these objectives, because the smoking of the tobacco has the effect of converting itself into a filthy and disgusting vice.

126. Frankincense must be used by all the devotees of the path.

127. Frankincense must be utilized in the moments of matrimonial vows, etc.

128. Devotion and veneration opens the doors of the superior worlds for the devotees of the path.

129. When we penetrate into the elemental temple of the olibanum trees, we see each one of the elemental children of these trees playing happily in the temple of frankincense...

130. These elementals use yellow tunics and their mantra is **"Alumino."**

131. We can invoke these elementals with this mantra, so that they can prepare the atmosphere of frankincense...
132. The angel who governs these elemental creatures resembles a bride clothed with a wedding dress...
133. Each one of these trees has its own elemental.
134. We will not tire of explaining that each plant and tree is a physical body of an elemental of nature who is preparing to one day enter into the animal kingdom and later into the human kingdom.
135. When we tear part of a tree or a plant, the elemental feels the same pain that we feel when one of our limbs is torn from our body.
136. Before taking a plant, a circle must be traced around it, and it must be blessed. We must then beg the elemental creature for the desired service.
137. A triangle must be traced around trailing plants. They must then be blessed, and then taken [read *Treatise of Esoteric Medicine and Practical Magic* by the same author].
138. The elemental creatures of the plants are totally innocent because they have not yet departed from Eden. They still have all the terrific powers of their seven igneous serpents.
139. We can invoke the elemental angel of the frankincense. He will concur to our call with the elemental creatures of the olibanum trees, in order to prepare the mystical environment of our Gnostic rituals.

Elemental Magic of Myrrh
COMMIPHORA MYRRHA

140. When we penetrate into the elemental department of the balsamum trees from which myrrh is extracted, we see these elemental children happy in Eden, dressed with incarnadine tunics and capes.
141. Myrrh belongs to spiritual gold and is associated with frankincense and with the gold of the spirit, like the ineffable pleroma of Nirvana.
142. The science of myrrh is the science of death.

143. There is a need to die in order to live.
144. There is a need to lose everything in order to gain everything.
145. There is a need to be dead to the world in order to be alive for God.
146. This is the elemental magic of the myrrh.

COMMIPHORA MYRRHA

147. The monadic essence of this elemental department of nature is intimately related with the world of the Innermost.
148. The spiritual gold is within the immense crucible of Nirvana.
149. The particular monads who constitute the monadic essence of each elemental department of nature are endowed with vehicles of a distinct density. Yet, even when they are particularized, we cannot say they are individualized, because they do not have an individual mind.
150. However, they are endowed with cosmic intelligence, innocence, power, and happiness.
151. The devas or angels are in charge of organizing the monadic essences, who are dressed with vehicles during this Mahamanvantara. These devas are their protectors and instructors. They perform their work as groups of spirits and are in charge of impelling the cosmic evolution of these monadic essences, who are known as elementals of nature and who are dressed with cosmic vehicles.
152. The monadic essences begin to show their own individuality when they pass through the evolution of the vegetable kingdom of nature.
153. We cannot say that the monad of a pine posteriorly reincarnated as a human being, but we can say that the monad of a human being was previously incarnated in a pine before becoming individualized as a human monad.

154. The monadic essences must evolve in the mineral, plant, and animal kingdoms before their individualization.

155. We cannot say that the monad of Descartes was incarnated in a tree, because the human monad is an individualized monad, different from the vegetable monad.

156. However, it is correct to affirm that the monad of Descartes was an animal monad, vegetable monad, and mineral monad before his individualization.

157. We understand that the monad is the Innermost of every mineral, vegetable, or animal elemental. The Innermost of the human being is composed of Atman-Buddhi-Manas.

158. The monads of the elementals of nature are totally impersonal beings.

159. The elementals of the myrrh are children of an enchanting beauty who possess the happiness of Nirvana.

160. Our disciples will now understand why gold, frankincense, and myrrh were offered to the God-Child of Bethlehem.

161. The arhat who learns how to handle the monadic essences of all the elemental departments of nature learns how to handle universal life.

162. The monadic essences of this great life emerge and reemerge incessantly with the great rhythms of the universal fire.

163. All these monadic essences reside in the profundity of the cosmic consciousness. We must learn how to handle them in order to work in this great laboratory of nature.

164. All the superlative spheres of the cosmic consciousness are classified by the *Vedas* in the following order:

165. **Atala** is the first plane, directly emanating from the Absolute. The hierarchies of the Dhyani Buddhas belong to this plane. They are in the state of parasamadhi or dharmakaya, a state in which there can be no progress, because they are completely perfect entities who only await the cosmic night in order to enter into the Absolute.

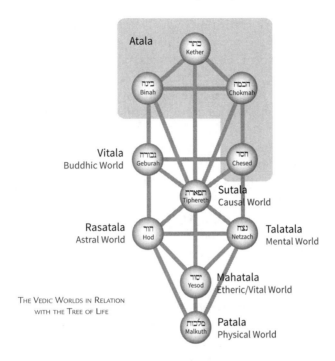

Atala

Kether — כתר

Binah — בינה   Chokmah — חכמה

Vitala
Buddhic World   Geburah — גבורה   Chesed — חסד

Tiphereth — תפארת   Sutala
Causal World

Rasatala
Astral World   Hod — הוד   Netzach — נצח   Talatala
Mental World

Yesod — יסוד   Mahatala
Etheric/Vital World

THE VEDIC WORLDS IN RELATION
WITH THE TREE OF LIFE

Malkuth — מלכות   Patala
Physical World

166. The second plane of the Vedas is **Vitala**. As it has been said, the celestial buddhas that have emanated from the seven Dhyani Buddhas are in this loka.

167. The third loka, or plane of consciousness, is **Sutala**. It is the plane of sound. Buddha Gautama reached that plane in this world. This is the plane of the hierarchies of the kumaras and agnishvattas.

168. The fourth loka of the Vedas is **Talatala**, the fifth is **Rasatala**, the sixth is **Mahatala**, and the seventh is **Patala**.

169. Atala is the world of the mist of fire, the world of the Innermost.

170. Vitala is the world of the consciousness. Sutala is the world of willpower. Talatala is the world of the mind. Rasatala is the astral world. Mahatala is the ethereal world and Patala is the physical world.

171. The monadic essences glow like virginal sparks in Atala. The sacred fire of our Lord Jesus Christ is in Vitala.

172. The elementals of the universal ether are in Sutala. The elementals of the fire are in Talatala.
173. The elementals of the air are in Rasatala. The aquatic elementals are in Mahatala. The humans, the elementals of animals and the gnomes are in Patala.
174. This classification is according to the old scriptures of the Vedas.
175. All of our seven cosmic planes are populated with elemental creatures.
176. The elemental creatures descend from the region of Atala to the physical world in order to evolve through the mineral, vegetable, animal, and human kingdoms.
177. The light descends plane by plane until reaching the physical world. It then ascends again to the ineffable region of Nirvana.
178. Everything comes and goes, emerges and reemerges, ascends and descends. Everything comes from Atala and returns to Atala in order to submerge itself in the end within the ineffable joy of the Absolute.
179. Myrrh belongs to the region of Atala, from where life descends in order to return and ascend anew.
180. Myrrh is the magic of the great alaya of the world.
181. The seven tattvas of nature are populated by elemental creatures and these creatures are incarnated in the plants.
182. One who learns how to handle vegetal magic can then handle the tattvas (read my *Treatise of Esoteric Medicine and Practical Magic*).
183. The Akashic tattva is the paradise of those virginal sparks who come from the monadic substances of the world of the Innermost.
184. The Vayu tattva is the element of the creatures who move the air.
185. The Tejas tattva is the element of the salamanders of the fire.
186. The Apas tattva is where the creatures of the water live.
187. The Prithvi tattva is the element in which the gnomes of the earth live.

188. All these innocent creatures are incarnated in the plants. One who knows the magic of the plants can then handle the tattvas of the universe.
189. We can calm the tempests, unleash the hurricanes, unleash the storms, and cause it to rain fire, as the prophet Elijah did, with the elementals of plants.
190. Myrrh is related with the Akasha that lives and palpitates in all which is created.

Elemental Magic of the Aloe
ALOE SUCCOTRINA

191. The aloe is a plant of great esoteric powers.
192. The elementals of this plant resemble newborn children.
193. These elemental children are true "Adamites" filled with innocent beauty.
194. This plant multiplies its leaves (pulpy leaves) without the necessity of the element earth or the element water.
195. I have often seen an aloe hanging upon a wall, without solar light and without water, inside of a room. The plant miraculously continues to live, reproducing its leaves and multiplying itself.

ALOE

196. How does it live? Upon what does it feed? What does it do in order to support itself?
197. Clairvoyant investigations have given us the logical conclusion that this plant lives and feeds itself with the ultra-sensitive rays of the sun.
198. This plant nourishes itself from the cosmic Christ, from the Christic rays of the sun.
199. The crystals of this plant become liquid sun, Christ in substance, Christonic semen.
200. The elementals of these plants have power over everything. We can utilize these elementals for any type of work of white magic, by means of its elemental magic.
201. Before taking the plant, water must be sprinkled upon it in order to baptize it.
202. The plant must then be blessed and the following Gnostic prayer must be recited.
203. **"I believe in the Son, the Cosmic Chrestos, the powerful astral mediator who links our physical personality with the supreme immanence of the Solar Father."**
204. A piece of silver must be hung upon the plant.
205. The plant must then be hung on the wall of our home. This is in order for the splendor of the Christic light (which the plant attracts from the sun) to illuminate and bathe the environment of our house, filling us with light and luck.
206. We can order the elemental of the aloe to execute the magical work that we desire by means of willpower. Thus, the elemental will immediately obey.
207. Indubitably, the orders must be given to the elemental daily, in order to command it to work.
208. The solar powers of this creature are tremendous. Nevertheless, whosoever intends to utilize the elemental creatures of nature for evil purposes will obtain a horrible karma and will be severely punished by the law.
209. The elementals of the aloe are intimately related with the laws of reincarnation.

210. The elemental department of the aloe is intimately related with the cosmic forces that take charge of regulating human reincarnation.

211. Just as the aloe can be pulled out from the earth in order to be hung upon the wall (in other words, its environment can be changed and it continues to live), just as well, the human being can also be pulled out from the earth and his environment changed in order to continue to live. This is the law of reincarnation.

212. We can even prove this law physically.

213. There is an insect called the cicada in the tropical forests.

214. It is a kind of hemipterous insect of a yellow-green color. The cicada produces a shrilling and monotonous singing noise in the heat of the summer by means of a particular organ that the male possesses in the inferior part of the abdomen.

215. In Colombia, the people give the common name of "chicharra" to this insect.

216. There is a common belief among these people that when singing this small animal bursts and dies. However, the reality is different.

217. What happens is that this animal abandons its "chitin" (organic substance that constitutes the skeleton of jointed animals).

218. The insect makes an opening in its dorsal thorax region and leaves through there, re-vested with a new body, full of life.

219. This tiny animal is immortal. It incessantly reincarnates itself in life.

220. The Master Huiracocha states the following about the aloe in his book entitled *Sacred Plants*, page 137, Argentinean edition, 1947:

221. "The travelers who go to the east will see a crocodile skin and an aloe plant above the doors in the Turkish houses. They say that both guarantee long life."

222. If this symbol is very carefully examined, then we find that it represents reincarnation.

223. *The Egyptian Book of the Dead* textually states:

224. *"I am the sacred crocodile Sebekh, I am the flame of three wicks and my wicks are immortal. I enter the region of Sekem, I enter the region of the flames that have defeated my adversaries."*

225. The sacred crocodile Sebekh symbolizes the Innermost. Therefore, if we place the aloe next to the crocodile, then we will have the Innermost with his three wicks, which symbolizes the divine triad reincarnating itself incessantly in order to reach perfection.

226. For some people, reincarnation is a belief. For others, it is a theory. For many, it is a superstition, etc. However, for those who remember their past lives, reincarnation is a fact.

227. I personally remember all my past lives, as naturally as I remember the hour in which I sit for lunch or dinner. All the wise people of the world could come to me and tell me that I am mistaken. However, I would simply laugh at them and look at them with compassion. For how could I forget that which I remember?

228. Reincarnation for me is a fact.

229. I knew the dawn of life upon the Earth, and I have been on this planet since the Polar Epoch.

230. I witnessed the departure from Eden, and I can assure you that the causa causorum of the loss of the inner powers of the human race was fornication.

231. The tribes of Lemuria lived on ranches. The soldiers of the tribes lived in their quarters.

232. The weapons of the soldiers were arrows and lances.

233. Only one entire tribe lived on a gigantic ranch.

234. Sexual relations were performed only on the huge patios of the temples during certain times of the year and under the orders of the angels.

235. However, the Lucifers awoke the thirst of passion within us, and we surrendered ourselves to fornication on these ranches.

236. I assisted in the departure from Eden. I witnessed the departure from paradise. This is why I testify all that I have seen and heard...

237. I still remember how when we fornicated we were cast out of the White Lodge.

238. When we ate the forbidden fruit, the great hierophants of Major Mysteries cast us from the patios of the temples.

239. Since that time, all the human beings have rolled through millions of births and deaths as numerous as the sands of the sea.

240. The plan of the angels was that as soon as the human being acquired a brain and a throat to speak, man and woman would then stop having sexual intercourse.

241. This was the plan of the angels, but the Lucifers ruined this plan. The human being then sank into the abyss.

242. A savior was sent for humanity, but truly, it is sad to say that human evolution has failed.

243. During the Polar and Hyperborean Epochs and in the beginning of Lemuria, we, the human beings were hermaphrodites. Reproduction was performed through "spores" that were separated from the calves.

244. The human being utilized the two poles of his sexual energy, positive and negative, in order to create through spores.

245. With the division into opposite sexes, the human being retained one pole of his sexual energy in order to form the brain and the throat.

246. Then, sexual cooperation was necessary for the reproduction of the race.

247. The sexual act was then performed under the direction of the angels, in determined periods of the year.

248. The plan of the angels was that as soon as the brain and the throat were constructed, humans would then continue their evolution by creating their body with the power of the Word.

249. I was a witness to all these things. This is why reincarnation for me is a fact.

250. I knew the tenebrous and tantric sexual magic that Mr. Cherenzi and Mr. Parsival (both black magicians) are preaching. I saw this black tantra being performed by all

the black magicians of Atlantis. This is why the continent of Atlantis was submerged amidst great cataclysms.

251. I knew the Egyptians and the Romans. I often saw Nero seated on his canopy bed upon the shoulders of his servants, while passing through the doors of the ancient Roman palace of the Caesars.

252. The human beings have been evolving through the wheels of birth and death for more than eighteen million years.

253. It is sad, very sad indeed, to say the truth, but this human evolution has truly failed.

254. A very small group of souls will reincarnate in the luminous Age of Aquarius.

255. I know the pseudo, theoretical spiritual devotees of the world very well, and with anticipation, I know that they will laugh at my affirmation and believe that I am ignorant... Poor people... I know all their theories by memory. I know all their libraries, and I can asseverate that a large part of the spiritual devotees of these societies, classrooms, orders, etc., walk on the black path.

256. It seems incredible, but we find truly luminous souls among humble peasants and simple people who have never devoured theories or "sepulchral food." These souls are millions of times more evolved than those sanctimonious ones who smile sweetly in the auditorium of all the parrot cages of the most established and profane schools of spiritualism.

257. The angels that direct the law of reincarnation are intimately related with this elemental department of the aloe.

258. The mantra of this elemental is the vowel "**M**."

259. The correct pronunciation of this vowel is made with the lips closed.

260. This sound is similar to the bellow of an ox.

261. However, I do not want to say that you have to imitate the ox.

262. When the sound is articulated it should be done with closed lips, then the sound will leave through the nose.

263. Every human being can remember his past lives by means of a retrospective exercise.

264. You can perform the retrospective exercise daily, in order to meticulously remember all the incidents that occurred the previous day, and to inversely remember all the events that occurred eight days before, fifteen days, one month, two months, one year, ten years, twenty years, etc., until precisely remembering all the events of the first years of our childhood.

265. During the retrospective exercise, when the student reaches the first three or four years of his childhood, then it is very difficult for him to remember the events of the first years of childhood.

266. However, when the student reaches this point, he should then practice the exercise during the transition between vigil and sleep.

267. Then, in visions during his dreams, he will meticulously remember all the details of his childhood, because when dreaming, we are in contact with the subconsciousness where all our memories are stored.

268. When we take advantage of the state of transition between vigil and sleep, this procedure of internal retrospection can be prolonged until we remember the instances that preceded the death of our past physical body, and the last painful scenes. While continuing the retrospective exercise, we continue to remember our entire past reincarnation and all the past reincarnations that preceded it.

269. This exercise of profound, internal, and delicate retrospection permits us to remember all our past lives.

Elemental Magic of the Storax Tree
STYRAX OFFICINALIS

270. The storax tree symbolizes wisdom and justice.

271. The mantra of this tree is "**Toliphando**."

272. The elemental department of the storax tree is found to be intimately related with the activities of karma.

273. The elemental department of the storax tree is directed by the lords of karma.
274. The lords of karma keep an exact note of all our debts in their books.
275. When we have capital to pay, and we pay, then we do well in business.
276. However, when we do not have capital to pay, we must inevitably pay with pain.
277. Perform good deeds so that you can pay your debts.
278. You not only pay karma for the evil that you have done, but also for the good that you should have done but did not do.
279. Love is law, but conscious love.
280. It is also possible to pay a lot of karma, to cancel many debts, by practicing sexual magic. This is because the blood of the lamb washes the sins of the world.
281. It is also possible to ask for credit from the lords of karma, but the credit must be paid with sacrifice for humanity.
282. All negotiations are arranged with the lords of karma by personally speaking with them in the internal worlds.

Elemental Magic of the Peppermint Plant
MENTHA PIPERITA

283. The elemental department of the peppermint is intimately related with the three runes AR, TYR, and MAN.

ᛅ ↑ ᛉ

284. The first rune AR represents God within man, the divine forces acting within the human being and the sacred altar of life.
285. The second rune TYR represents the divine Trinity, reincarnating itself through the wheel of births and deaths.
286. The third rune MAN represents the human being.
287. The governing angel of the mint helps us to pass from the darkness into the light.

288. The hierarchies related with the elemental department of the peppermint act by leading the reincarnating souls through the narrow way that arrives to the womb.

289. The divine hierarchies of the peppermint plant synthesize their activities in the three runes IS, RITA, and GIBOR.

I ᚱ ᚷ

290. IS represents the phallus in which all the power of the sexual force is enclosed.

291. RITA represents the rose that symbolizes divine justice.

292. GIBOR represents the letter "G" of generation.

293. The activity of great beings is related with the elemental department of the peppermint and is based on these three fundamental letters.

294. The angels who are related with the elemental department of the peppermint wisely direct the entire scientific process of reincarnation, the entire biological process of fetal conception.

295. The passage that the masculine sperm travels in the narrow fallopian tubes is very similar to the straight and narrow passage that leads from the darkness into the light.

296. In the ancient temples of the mysteries, the neophyte reached the altar of the temple after he passed through a narrow and straight passage that led him from the darkness into the light.

297. The hierarchies related with the peppermint scientifically direct all of the biological processes of the reproduction of the race, according to cosmic justice.

298. The governing angel of this elemental department of nature wisely leads us through the narrow passage of the temples of the mysteries to the altar of illumination.

299. The peppermint is intimately related with the Akashic records of nature.

300. The mantras of the peppermint permit us to remember our past reincarnations.

301. These mantras are "**Raom Gaom**." These mantras can be vocalized mentally during the retrospection exercises performed in profound meditation, in order to remember our past lives.

302. The mantras Raom Gaom permit us to open the closed records of nature's memory in order to remember our past reincarnations.

303. This is the elemental magic of the peppermint.

304. Many disciples will find it unusual and even strange that I relate the peppermint to the law of reincarnation and with the biological processes of human conception.

305. On page 294 of the first volume of *The Secret Doctrine*, H.P. Blavatsky cites Hermes Trismegistus as stating:

306. *"The creation of life by the sun is as continuous as his light; nothing arrests or limits it.*

    "Around him, like an army of satellites, are innumerable choirs of genii.

    "These dwell in the neighborhood of the Immortals, and thence watch over human things.

    "They fulfill the will of the gods (karma) by means of storms, tempests, transitions of fire and earthquakes; likewise by famines and wars, for the punishment of impiety.

    "It is the sun who preserves and nourishes all creatures: and even as the ideal world which environs the sensible world fills this last with the plenitude and universal variety of forms, so also the Sun, enfolding all in his light, accomplishes everywhere the birth and development of creatures.

    "Under his orders is the choir of genii, or rather the choirs, for there are many and diverse, and their number corresponds to that of the stars.

    "Every star has its genii, good and evil by nature, or rather by their operation, for operation is the essence of the genii.

    "All of these genii preside over mundane affairs.

307. *"They shake and overthrow the constitution of states and of individuals; they imprint their likeness on our souls, they are present*

*in our nerves, our marrow, our veins, our arteries, and our very
brain-substance.*

*"At the moment when each one of us receives life and
being, he is taken in charge by the genii (elementals)
who preside over births, and who are classed beneath
the astral powers (superhuman astral spirits).*

*"They change perpetually, not always identically, but
revolving in circles[progressive cycles in development].*

*"They permeate by the body two parts of the soul, that it
may receive from each the impress of his own energy.*

*"But the reasonable part of the soul is not subject to the
genii. It is designed for the reception of (the) God [the
Innermost] who enlightens it with a sunny ray.*

*"Those who are thus illumined are few in number, and
from them the genii abstain (this is how the human beings
liberate themselves from karma): for neither genii nor gods
have any power in the presence of a single ray of God.*

*"But all other men, both soul and body, are directed by genii,
to whom they cleave, and whose operations they affect.*

*"The genii have then the control of mundane things
and our bodies serve them as instruments..."*

308. These elemental genii of nature are known in India as
bhuts, devas, shaitans, and djinn.
309. All these great beings are children from the mist of the
fire. They are the Army of the Voice. They are perfect
beings.
310. Everything that exists in the universe has sprouted from
its seed.
311. The seeds of everything that exist are the monadic
essences of the mist of the fire.
312. When the heart of the solar system began to palpitate
after the great cosmic night, the "devouring" atoms of
the mist of the fire dispersed all the atoms of the monadic essences, in order for the elemental life of the four
kingdoms of nature to emerge from them.

313. Each atom of nature is the body of a virginal spark that incessantly evolves through time and space.
314. These virginal sparks are the divine monads that constitute the seed plot of the cosmos.
315. These virginal sparks, when united, are called monadic essences.
316. Each one of the atoms of our physical body and our internal bodies are the living incarnation of these virginal sparks.
317. All the virginal sparks evolve and progress under the direction of the angels.
318. Our disciples will now understand why the angels of the peppermint direct all the processes of fetal conception and reproduction of the races.
319. There are three aspects of cosmic evolution that are found mixed and entwined everywhere upon our earth.
320. These three aspects are monadic evolution, mental evolution and physical evolution.
321. However, the monadic essences are the fundamental base of mental and physical development in the processes of evolution.
322. As long as the monadic essences are evolving, all of great nature is transforming.
323. Each one of these three evolving currents is directed and governed by various groups of Dhyanis or Logoi.
324. These groups of divine beings are found represented in our entire human constitution.
325. That which is called "human being" is constituted by the monadic current in union with the evolving wave of the mind and with the evolution of the physical body. The evolving wave of the mind is represented by the manasa-dhyanis (the solar devas or pitris-agnishvatta). The evolution of the physical body is represented by the chhayas from the lunar pitris.
326. Nature, the evolving physical power, can never acquire consciousness or intelligence without the help of these divine angels.

327. The manasa-dhyanis are the ones who endow the human being with mind and intelligence.

328. Each virginal atom of the mineral kingdom is the physical body of a divine monad, who aspires to become human.

329. We read the following comment from page 183 of the first volume of *The Secret Doctrine*, by H.P. Blavatsky:

330. *"Every form on earth, and every speck (atom) in the space strives in its efforts towards self-formation to follow the model placed for it in the "heavenly man."*

   "Its (the atom's) involution and evolution, its external and internal growth and development, have all one and the same object-man; man, as the highest physical and ultimate form on this earth; the monad, in its absolute totality and awakened condition--as the culmination of the divine incarnations on Earth."

331. All the animal, vegetable, and mineral elementals will convert themselves into human beings during the periods of Jupiter, Venus, and Vulcan.

332. To synthesize, all four of our inferior bodies are formed by atomic elementals or atomic consciousness, governed by devas or angels of nature.

333. Our individual life is totally related with the universal life.

334. The internal life of the plants is within ourselves.

335. As well, the region of the distinct elemental departments of nature is within ourselves, directing our biological processes and all of our conscious and mental processes.

336. The four seasons of the year are within ourselves. They repeat themselves in our internal consciousness.

337. Therefore, it is impossible to separate our life from the great ocean of the universal life. With a simple herb we can often free the tempests or make the earth tremble, because the life of an insignificant herb is united with all the lives of this great universal life.

338. Force and forces are always united in creation.

339. The life of each one of the plants of nature is repeated within ourselves, and the total sum of all these additions constitutes that which is called the human being.

Elemental Magic of the Fig Tree
FICUS CARICA OR FICUS COMMUNIS

340. *"And when he saw a fig tree in the way, he came to it, and found nothing thereon, but leaves only, and said unto it, Let no fruit grow on thee henceforward for ever. And presently the fig tree withered away."* —Matthew 21:19

341. The elemental department of the fig tree belongs to the sexual forces.

342. The mantra of the elementals of the fig trees is "**Afiras.**"

343. The hierarchies related with this elemental department of nature are those who apply karma to fornicators.

344. Fornicators are cast into the burning lake of fire and sulphur. This is the second death.

345. *"...Every tree therefore which bringeth not forth good fruit is hewn down and cast into the fire."* —Luke 3:9

346. The grandiose power of the sexual force resides in the Kundalini.

347. There are seven cosmic forces:

348. First: the force of the **Glorian.**

Second: **Para-shakti** (light and heat).

Third: **Jnana-shakti** (wisdom, intelligence).

Fourth: **Iccha-shakti** (willpower).

Fifth: **Kriya-shakti** (Christic-mind)

Sixth: **Kundalini-shakti** (seven serpents)

Seventh: **Mantrika-shakti** (the power of the Word).

349. All of the seven cosmic forces are enclosed within the Kundalini Shakti, and the Kundalini is enclosed within the sexual force of the virile member and the feminine vulva.

350. The secret for awakening the Kundalini is enclosed within the union of the phallus and the uterus.

351. The Kundalini evolves and progresses within the aura of the Solar Logos.
352. The evolution of the six remaining forces depends on the evolution of the Kundalini.
353. All the power of the mind, all the power of light and heat, all the power of the Word and willpower are enclosed within the sacred serpent, whose power resides in the phallus and the uterus.
354. *"...Every tree therefore which bringeth not forth good fruit is hewn down and cast into the fire."* —Luke 3:9
Fornicators are sterile fig trees who are hewn down and cast into the fire.
355. The fig tree symbolizes the feminine sexual forces that we must learn how to control.
356. The rooster and the fig tree represent the sexual forces.
357. This is why the rooster of Christ's Passion cannot be absent from the drama of Calvary.
358. The fig tree solely represents the feminine sexual forces.
359. It is impossible to reach deep realization without the alchemy of the feminine solar forces.
360. Christ, in His dignity as Cosmic Christ, said, *"I am the door and by me if any man enter in, he shall be saved, and shall go in and out, and find pasture."* —John 10:9
361. The Christonic substance of the savior of the world is placed in our Christonic semen. This is why the door that enters into Eden is in our sexual organs.
362. We transmute the Christonic semen into a subtle Christic energy. Thus, within our astral body we form a sublime vehicle, a superior astral body, which is the I-Christ, by means of sexual alchemy (read our book *Treatise of Sexual Alchemy*).
363. The I-Christ, which is formed with the same essence of the savior of the world, is the door entering into the great mysteries of the fire.
364. The mysteries of the fire are known only by entering through the door of Eden.

365. It is completely impossible to enter into the great mysteries of the mind without previously forming the I-Christ within our astral body (read our book *The Seven Words*).

366. Christ and Jehovah must be formed within us in order to penetrate into the great initiations of the fire.

367. Jehovah is the Holy Spirit within us, who is the result of the incessant transformations of our Christonic semen.

368. Christ and Jehovah live within us as seminal substances.

369. The illumination of the masters comes from the Holy Spirit.

370. The Lord Jehovah is the Holy Spirit within us, whose omniscience illuminates us internally.

371. We must form Christ and Jehovah in order to enter into Nirvana.

372. All the esoteric powers of the master come from the Christic substance and from the illumination of the Holy Spirit within ourselves.

373. However, we must not forget that in our inner depth each one of us is a star.

374. The star that burns within us is the Father, whose divine individuality we must absorb, in order to complete the perfect, divine Trinity.

375. There is the need to form the Father, the Son, and the Holy Spirit within ourselves.

376. Christ and Jehovah reside within us as seminal substances.

377. The Lord Jehovah is formed within us with the transmutations of the semen.

378. The omniscient powers of the adept are enclosed within the Holy Spirit.

379. The Lord Jehovah is a divine entity, filled with omniscience and power.

380. The substance of the Lord Jehovah and the Christonic substance of the Solar Logos are dispersed everywhere.

381. To form the Lord Jehovah within us is to form the Holy Spirit within us.

382. The Holy Spirit gives the master wisdom and magical powers.

383. Therefore, the Lord Jehovah and the Lord Christ are individual entities and cosmic essences that are stored within the semen.

384. It is infinitely lamentable that in this present epoch there are no advanced esotericists that can explain who the Lord Jehovah is.

385. Max Heindel committed the error of considering the Lord Jehovah as a divine entity of the past.

386. H.P. Blavatsky considered Jehovah as Ilda-Baoth, a name composed of Ilda, meaning "child," and Baoth, meaning "of an egg and the Chaos, Void or Desolation"; or "the child born from the egg and the Chaos." According to Blavatsky, Jehovah, like Brahma, is simply one of the Elohim, one of the seven creative spirits and one of the inferior Sephiroth.

387. In reality, this very vague explanation that H. P. Blavatsky and Max Heindel give regarding Jehovah fails to fill the longing of the soul.

388. Huiracocha believes that Jehovah is only the five vowels I-E-O-U-A, which is perfectly absurd.

389. It is very good that we relate JOHN with the five vowels I-E-O-U-A. But Jehovah is something different. Jehovah is a divine entity. Jehovah is transmuted semen. Jehovah is the Holy Spirit within ourselves.

390. The divine Rabbi of Galilee, when speaking of the Holy Spirit, tells us the following:

"And I say unto you, Ask, and it shall be given you; seek, and ye shall find; knock, and it shall be opened unto you.

"For every one that asketh receiveth; and he that seeketh findeth; and to him that knocketh it shall be opened.

"If a son shall ask bread of any of you that is a father, will he give him a stone? or if he ask a fish, will he for a fish give him a serpent?

"Or if he shall ask an egg, will he offer him a scorpion?

*"If ye then being evil, know how to give good gifts unto your
children: how much more shall your heavenly Father give
the Holy Spirit to them that ask him?"* —Luke 11:9-13

391. All of the magical powers of the master are due to the
Holy Spirit.

392. The Holy Spirit gives us wisdom and magical powers.

393. The Holy Spirit is pure, transmuted semen.

394. When the Kundalini reaches the Brahmarandra and
leaves towards the exterior world through the frontal
fontanel of the newborn child, it assumes the mystical figure of the white dove of the Holy Spirit with His
omniscient atoms. The white dove then floats within the
blaze of the sacred fire.

395. This white dove confers wisdom and magical powers to
the adept.

396. Since the dawn of life on this planet, these selected
atoms of the Kundalini, which form the Holy Spirit within ourselves, were placed in our Christonic semen by the
Lord Jehovah.

397. Just as we carry the blood of our Father within our veins,
likewise we carry in our semen the sacred essences of
Christ, Jehovah and the Father.

398. We form the I-Christ with the Christic substance, and
with him we replace the "animal I."

399. We form the Holy Spirit within ourselves with the seminal substance of Jehovah, and with Him we acquire esoteric wisdom and divine powers.

400. We strengthen the Innermost with the seminal substance
of the Father in order to form the Father within ourselves.

401. This is how we form the Father, the Son, and the Holy
Spirit within ourselves, and we are converted into terrific,
divine majesties of the universe.

402. All the mysteries of electricity, magnetism, polarities,
light, and heat are found enclosed within our sexual
organs.

403. The septenary of the entire human being is totally
absorbed within our eternal triad.

404. The entire septenary remains synthesized in the divine triad: Atman-Buddhi-Manas.

405. The I-Christ is absorbed in the superlative consciousness of the Being, in the diamond soul, in Buddhi.

406. The Holy Spirit within ourselves is absorbed in the body of willpower, superior manas, or causal body.

407. The pure seminal essence of the Father is absorbed in the Innermost, in order to form the Father within ourselves.

408. This is how the human septenary remains reduced to a perfect triad, whose vehicle of concrete expression is the human bodhisattva (the astral body of the master).

409. In the east, they say that the buddhas are double.

410. There is the heavenly man and the earthly man.

411. There are the earthly buddhas and the buddhas of contemplation.

412. Fifty years after the death of Buddha, he sent his human soul or Holy Spirit to the Earth, enclosed and absorbed in his superior manas, in order to again incarnate and to complete his mission.

413. This mission was accomplished by his bodhisattva, under the direction of Shankaracharya.

414. Shankara was a ray of the primitive light; he was a flame.

415. Shankara joined the Buddhist doctrine with the Advaita philosophy.

416. This is how the astral bodhisattva of Buddha completed the mission of his internal master.

417. A bodhisattva is formed by the Holy Spirit of a master dressed with the four lower bodies.

418. This is the greatest mystery of the human personality.

419. This is the mystery of the double human personality. This is one of the greatest mysteries of esotericism.

420. The internal master can send his Holy Spirit to the Earth clothed with a mental, astral, vital and physical body in order to perform an important mission.

421. Christ, the divine redeemer of the world, after his earthly death, sent his human bodhisattva. But the human beings knew him not.

THE BUDDHA, THE SEVEN SERPENTS, AND THE SACRED FIG TREE

422. However, in the Age of Aquarius, the Christic triad will reincarnate in an integral form in order to teach Christic esotericism to humanity.
423. The Gnostic movement will then give its fruits, and the entire Aquarian humanity will be prepared to understand the last explanations of the master.
424. There is the need to distinguish between what the avatars are and what the savior is.
425. John the Baptist was the avatar of Pisces and I am the avatar of Aquarius.
426. The savior of the world is not an avatar. He is more than all of the avatars. He is the savior.
427. We, the avatars, are simply the instructors and the founders of a new era.
428. Christ is more than all the instructors. He is the savior.
429. The hierarchies related with the elemental department of the fig tree are responsible for applying karma to all evil ones, sodomites, and to all sexually degenerated ones who are so abundant in this humanity.
430. The name of the governing angel of this elemental department of nature is "Najera."
431. The elementals of this elemental department of the fig tree use white tunics, and are children of extraordinary beauty.
432. The white tunic represents chastity and sanctity.
433. The members of all the spiritual schools hate chastity and they skillfully avoid it by searching for an escape through the false door of their theories.
434. Their same weakness, their same lack of willpower, causes them to search for subtle escapes in order to avoid the problem of chastity.
435. Some of them even begin to practice sexual magic, but they suddenly succumb because of the lustful demands of their fornicating spouses.
436. Therefore, we the Gnostics affirm, "Our motto is THE-LE-MA (willpower)."
437. All the spiritual henchmen of fornication are black magicians because they are disobeying the commandment

which was given by the Lord Jehovah, as stated in the following verses:

438. *"And the Lord Jehovah commanded the man, saying, of every tree of the garden thou mayest freely eat: But of the tree of the knowledge of good and evil, thou shall not eat of it: for in the day that thou eatest thereof thou shall surely die."* —Genesis 2:16-17

439. Therefore, the perverse henchmen of all the pseudo-spiritualism and mystic theorizers from worldly intellectualism will not tread over this command of the Lord Jehovah.

440. The command of the Lord Jehovah must be fulfilled, no matter what the cost might be.

441. Fornicators are sterile fig trees and *"...Every tree therefore which bringeth not forth good fruit is hewn down and cast into the fire."* —Luke 3:9

Chapter 16

The Mind and Sexuality

1. All that has been written about the mind are only preliminary steps towards the sacred study of the igneous rose.
2. Vivekananda is one who has spoken more clearly about the mind. However, his teachings are scarcely preliminary notions towards the serious study of our mind.
3. The mind is intimately related with sexuality. It is impossible to study the mind without studying the sexual matter.
4. There are innumerable number of students who are dedicated to yoga and to the teachings of Krishnamurti. However, they achieve nothing and waste their time lamentably, because these poor beings are incessantly fornicating.
5. It is impossible to separate the mind from sexuality. The mind and sexuality are intimately related. If our disciples want to convert the material-mind into Christ-mind, then they must fill their chalice (brain) with the sacred wine of the light (semen).
6. It is impossible to Christify the mind while we are fornicating.
7. There is the need to practice sexual magic intensely in order to transform the mind.
8. We fill our mind with transformative atoms of a higher voltage by means of sexual magic.
9. This is how we prepare our mental body for the advent of the fire.
10. When the igneous serpent of the mental body has converted the material-mind into the Christ-mind, we then liberate ourselves from the four bodies of sin.
11. However, our single disciples can achieve great realizations with the terrific force of sacrifice.
12. Sexual abstinence is a tremendous sacrifice.
13. Francis of Assisi totally Christified himself by means of the force of sacrifice.

14. Bachelors must unite their willpower and imagination in vibrating harmony, and concentrate them on their sexual glands. Thus, they will cause their sexual force to rise from their sexual glands towards the brain by following the course of their spinal column.

15. They must then direct their sexual energy to the middle-brow, the neck, and then the heart, in successive order.

16. During this practice, our disciples must sing the following mantras:

17. **Kandil Bandil Rrrrrrr.**

18. These mantras must be vocalized in the following manner: KAN, resounding voice; DIL, decreasing voice. BAN resounding voice; DIL decreasing voice. The letter "R" is pronounced in a prolonged and high pitched form, imitating the sound produced by the rattle of the rattlesnake.

19. These are the most powerful mantras known in the entire infinite for the awakening of the Kundalini.

20. Male disciples who cannot practice sexual magic with their priestess wives, due to circumstances against their will, must then vow to eternal chastity and must not touch a woman for all of eternity.

21. Our single female disciples must perform the same practices of sexual transmutation that we have given to our single male disciples.

22. Our married female disciples must practice sexual magic with their husbands.

23. When they cannot practice sexual magic with their husbands, due to circumstances against their will, they must then completely abstain in order to awaken the Kundalini with the force of sacrifice and they must practice the key of transmutation that I have given for bachelors.

24. Every flame needs fuel in order to burn.

25. The sacred flame of our candlestick also has its fuel. This fuel is our oil of gold. It is our Christonic semen.

26. The human being who wastes his sacred oil cannot light his candlestick.

27. *"And the angel that talked with me came again, and waked me, as a man that is wakened out of his sleep.*

   "And said unto me, What seest thou? And I said, I have looked, and behold a candlestick all of gold, with a bowl upon the top of it, and his seven lamps thereon, and seven pipes to the seven lamps, which are upon the top thereof:

   "And two olive trees by it, one upon the right side of the bowl, and the other upon the left side thereof." —Zachariah 4:1-3

28. *"Then answered I, and said unto him, What are these two olive trees upon the right side of the candlestick and upon the left side thereof?*

   "And I answered again, and said unto him, What be these two olive branches which through the two golden pipes empty the golden oil out of themselves?

   "And he answered me and said, Knowest thou not what these be? And I said, No, my lord.

   "Then said he, These are the two anointed ones, that stand by the Lord of the whole earth." —Zachariah 4:11-14

29. These two anointed ones that stand by the Lord of the whole earth are our two ganglionic nerves that are entwined in our spinal column. We must make our seminal energy rise to the brain through these nerves.

30. May the Holy Grail be with us. May our chalice be filled with the blood of the Lamb.

31. This is how our mind is Christified.

32. It is impossible to Christify the mind without the fire.

33. Our disciples will now comprehend why the word "INRI" was placed above the head of the crucified one.

34. This word signifies, "Ignis Natura Renovatur Integra" (the fire renews nature incessantly).

35. The concept of Descartes, "I think, therefore I am," is completely false, because the true man is the Innermost, and the Innermost does not think, because He knows.

36. The mind thinks, not the Innermost.

37. In its current state of evolution, the human mind is the animal that we carry within.

38. The Innermost does not need to think because He is omniscient.

39. Our Innermost is *Yes, Yes, Yes.*

40. The wisdom of our Innermost is *Yes, Yes, Yes.*

41. The love of our Innermost is *Yes, Yes, Yes.*

42. When we say: "I am hungry, I am thirsty," etc., we are affirming something absurd, because the Innermost is not hungry, nor thirsty. The one who is hungry and thirsty is the physical body.

43. It is much better to say, "My body is hungry, my body is thirsty."

44. The same happens with the mind when we say, "I have a mental force, I have a strong mental force, I have a problem, I have such a conflict, I have such suffering, such thoughts are occurring to me," etc.

45. We are then affirming very grave errors, because these are things from the mind, not from the Innermost.

46. The Innermost has no problems. Problems are from the mind.

47. The true human being is the Innermost.

48. The Innermost must flagellate the mind with the terrific whip of willpower.

49. The one who identifies with the mind falls into the abyss.

50. The mind is a donkey upon which we must ride in order to enter into the heavenly Jerusalem.

51. We must command the mind like this, "Mind, take this problem away from me. Mind, take this conflict away from me. Mind, take this desire away from me, etc., etc. I do not accept it from you. I am your lord and you are my slave forevermore, until the consummation of the centuries."

52. Woe to the one who identifies with the mind, because he loses the Innermost and goes down into the abyss.

53. Those who say that everything is mind commit a very grave error, because the mind is only an instrument of the Innermost.

54. All writings that incline the human being to totally identify himself with the mind are legitimate black magic, because the true human being is not the mind.

55. We must not forget that the most sly and dangerous demons in the universe reside in the mental plane.

56. Therefore, the Innermost says this to the mind, "Do not say that your eyes are your eyes, because I see through them. Do not say that your ears are your ears, because I hear through them. Do not say that your mouth is your mouth, because I talk through it. Your eyes are my eyes, your ears are my ears, your mouth is my mouth."

57. This is how the Innermost speaks to the mind.

58. In the internal worlds, we can throw the mental body out of ourselves in order to speak with it face to face, as if it is a stranger.

59. We can then deeply comprehend that the mind is a strange subject that we must learn to control with the terrific whip of willpower.

60. The most perfect chastity is fundamentally necessary in order to Christify the mental body.

61. The den of desire is in the mind.

62. Persons who feel incapable of stopping fornication must speak to the mind like this, "Mind, take this sexual thought away from me; mind take this carnal desire away from me. You are my slave, and I am your lord."

63. Then, the horrible wolf of carnal passion will run away from the den of the mind, and those persons will acquire perfect chastity.

64. The mental donkey must be flagellated with the terrific whip of willpower.

65. It is impossible to separate the mind from sexuality. The mind and sexuality are intimately related. If our disciples want to convert the material-mind into Christ-mind, they must fill their chalice with the sacred wine of the light.

66. When the mind is completely Christified, it then converts itself into a splendid and marvelous vehicle with

which we can study all the secrets of this igneous rose of
the universe.

67. The Christ-mind is the most precious instrument of the
arhat.

Chapter 17
Esoteric Discipline of the Mind

1. Meditation is the esoteric discipline of the Gnostics.
2. Meditation has three steps: concentration, meditation, and samadhi.
3. Concentration means to fix the mind on only one object. Meditation means to reflect upon the substantial contents of that one object. Samadhi is ecstasy, mystical joy.
4. A master of samadhi penetrates all the planes of consciousness, and with the Eye of Dangma he investigates all the secrets of the wisdom of the fire.
5. It is urgent for our Gnostic disciples to learn how to function without any type of material vehicles so that they can perceive all the marvels of the universe with the Eye of Dangma.
6. This is how our disciples will convert themselves into masters of samadhi.
7. The disciple must profoundly meditate on his physical body while lying down on his bed with his hands crossed over his chest. He will tell himself: "I am not this physical body."
8. The disciple must then profoundly meditate on his ethereal body, telling himself: "I am not this ethereal body."
9. Then, submerged in profound internal meditation, the disciple must reflect on his astral body, and must say: "I am not the astral body."
10. The disciple must now meditate on his mental body and must say to himself: "Neither am I this mind with which I am thinking."
11. The disciple must then reflect on his willpower, and must tell himself: "Neither am I this body of willpower."
12. The disciple must now meditate in his consciousness, and must say to himself: "Neither am I the consciousness."

13. Now, at last, submerged in profound meditation, the disciple must exclaim in his heart: "I am the Innermost, I am the Innermost, I am the Innermost."

14. Once out of all his vehicles, the disciple will then be an indivisible majesty of the infinite.

15. He will then see that he does not need to think because the wisdom of the Innermost is: *Yes, Yes, Yes.*

16. The disciple will now be aware that the action of the Innermost is: *Yes, Yes, Yes.*

17. The disciple will now understand that the nature of the Innermost is absolute happiness, absolute existence, and absolute omniscience.

18. In these instances of supreme happiness, past and future join within an eternal now. The great cosmic days and the great cosmic nights are taking place, one after the other, within an eternal instant.

19. In this plenitude of happiness our disciples can study all the wisdom of the fire within the blazing flames of the universe.

20. This is how our disciples learn to function without any material vehicles, in order to study all the secrets of the elemental magic of nature.

21. There is the necessity for the Innermost to learn how to undress Himself in order to function without vehicles in the great alaya of the world.

22. Concentration, meditation, and samadhi are the three obligatory paths for initiation.

23. First of all, attention is fixed on the body with which we want to practice. Then, we meditate on its internal constitution, and filled with mystical joy we say: "I am not this body."

24. Concentration, meditation, and samadhi must be practiced on each body.

25. Concentration, meditation, and samadhi are known in the East as samyama. We must perform it on each one of our vehicles.

26. In order to divest each one of our inferior vehicles, we must practice a samyama on each one of our vehicles.

27. The great ascetics of meditation are the great sannyasis of the cosmic mind, whose flames glow within the igneous rose of the universe.

28. It is urgent to acquire absolute chastity, tenacity, serenity and patience in order to be a sannyasin of the mind.

29. After a certain time of practice, our disciples can liberate themselves from all of their six vehicles in order to function in the great alaya of the universe without any kind of vehicles.

30. The disciple will notice that his dreams become clearer day by day. He will then comprehend that when his physical body sleeps, the internal man travels, acts, and works within the supra-sensible worlds.

31. The disciple will now understand that so-called dreams are living experiences in the internal worlds.

32. Our head is a tower with two rooms, the cerebrum and the cerebellum.

33. The cerebellum is the room of the subconsciousness. The cerebrum is the room of the consciousness.

34. The wisdom of the internal worlds belongs to the room of the subconsciousness. The things of our world belong to the room of the consciousness.

35. When the consciousness and the subconsciousness are united, one can then study all the marvels of the internal worlds and pass them to the physical brain.

36. It is urgent that our disciples join the two rooms of this marvelous tower of our head.

37. The key for this is the retrospective exercise.

38. When we awake after our dream, we must practice a retrospective exercise. This is in order to remember all the things that we saw and heard and all the works that we performed when we were out, far from the physical body.

39. This is how the two rooms of the consciousness and the subconsciousness are joined in order to give us great illumination.

40. There are no false dreams. Every dream is a living experience in the internal worlds.

41. Even the so-called nightmares are real experiences, because the monsters of nightmares truly exist in the submerged worlds.

42. Indigestion can put certain chakras of the lower abdomen into activity. We then penetrate into the atomic infernos of the human being where, truly, the most monstrous beings of the universe live. This is what is called nightmares.

43. The images of the supra-sensible worlds are totally symbolic. There is a need to learn how to interpret them, basing ourselves in the law of philosophical analogies, in the law of analogies of the opposites, in the law of correspondences, and the law of numerology.

44. Even the most apparently absurd dreams enclose the greatest revelation, if they are wisely interpreted.

45. Our disciples must not move themselves at the time of awakening, because with this movement, the astral body is agitated and the memories are lost.

46. As soon as he awakes on his bed, the disciple first needs to practice the retrospective exercise in order to remember with precision all of his internal experiences. This is how internal wisdom is attained, when the two rooms of the consciousness and the subconsciousness are united.

47. The samnyasin of thought achieves continuous consciousness within the igneous rose of the universe.

48. It is necessary to achieve the most profound serenity. It is urgent to develop patience and tenacity.

49. There is the need to remain indifferent before praise and slander, before triumph and failure.

50. It is necessary to change the process of reasoning for the beauty of comprehension.

51. It is indispensable to make an addition of all our defects and dedicate two months to each defect, until eliminating all defects.

52. Whosoever intends to eliminate all defects at the same time is similar to the hunter that wants to hunt ten hares at the same time. He does not succeed in hunting any of them.

53. In order to become a master of samadhi, it is urgent to cultivate a rich interior life.

54. The Gnostic who does not know how to smile has less control of himself, like the one who only knows the guffaw of Aristophanes.

55. There is the need to achieve complete control of ourselves. An initiate can feel happiness, but he will never fall into the frenzy of madness. An initiate can feel sadness, but he will never reach desperation.

56. He who is desperate about the death of a beloved being still does not serve as an initiate, because death is the crown of everyone.

57. During the practice of meditation, the chakras of our disciples' astral body enter into activity. Disciples then begin to perceive the images of the supra-sensible worlds.

58. In the beginning, the disciple perceives fleeting images. Later, the disciple totally perceives all the images of the supra-sensible worlds.

59. This first stage of knowledge belongs to 'imaginative' knowledge.

60. The disciple contemplates many images that are mysteries for him because he does not understand them.

61. Yet, as long as he perseveres with his practices of internal meditation, he will then feel that the supra-sensible images produce certain feelings of happiness or pain.

62. The disciple then feels inspired in the presence of the internal images. He has thus risen to the stage of inspired knowledge.

63. Later, when he sees an internal image, instantaneously he knows its significance and the reason for many things. This is the third stage of knowledge, known as intuitive knowledge.

64. Imagination, Inspiration, and Intuition are the three obligatory paths for initiation.

65. We reach these three ineffable heights by means of concentration, meditation and samadhi.

66. Whosoever has reached these ineffable heights of intuition has converted himself into a master of samadhi.

67. Asian wisdom practices meditation in the following order:

     1. **Asana** (posture of the body).

     2. **Pratyahara** (thinking in nothing).

     3. **Dharana** (concentration on only one thing).

     4. **Dhyana** (profound meditation).

     5. **Samadhi** (ecstasy).

68. It is necessary to place the body in the most comfortable position (asana).

     It is indispensable to empty the mind before concentrating (pratyahara).

     It is urgent to know how to fix the mind on only one object (dharana).

     Then, we profoundly reflect on the content of the object itself (dhyana).

     Thus, in this way, we reach ecstasy (samadhi).

69. All of these esoteric disciplines of the mind must completely saturate our daily life.

70. In the presence of any person, many images that correspond to the internal life of that person with whom we are in contact will emerge from our interior. This is known as clairvoyance.

71. Later, these images produce distinct feelings of inspiration within ourselves. The disciple has then reached the stage of inspired knowledge.

72. Finally, in the presence of any person, the disciple instantaneously knows the life of that person. This is the stage of intuitive knowledge.

73. Those who want to enter into the wisdom of the fire must overcome the process of reasoning and cultivate the ardent faculties of the mind.

74. We must only extract the golden fruit from reasoning.

75. The golden fruit of reasoning is comprehension.

76. Comprehension and imagination must replace reasoning.

77. Imagination and comprehension are the foundation of the superior faculties of the mind.

78. In order to enter into the knowledge of the superior worlds, it is necessary to acquire the superior faculties of the mind.

79. Those who read the teachings of *The Igneous Rose* and yet stubbornly continue to be enclosed in the process of reasoning do not serve for the superior studies of the spirit. Such individuals are not yet mature.

80. Clairvoyance and imagination are the same. Clairvoyance is imagination and imagination is clairvoyance. Clairvoyance exists eternally.

81. When an image emerges in our interior, it is then necessary to serenely examine it in order to know its contents.

82. When the igneous rose of our astral body (situated in the middlebrow) awakens into new activity, then the images that come internally to our imagination are accompanied with light and color.

83. It is necessary to learn by direct experience how to differentiate between the images that are received and the images that we consciously or unconsciously create or project.

84. It is necessary to differentiate between our own images and the outer images that come to us.

85. The imagination has two poles, one being a receptor and the other a projector.

86. Receiving an image is one thing. Projecting an image created by our mind is another thing.

87. The contrary pole of the imagination is [all that is] imaginary [fantasy].

88. Imagination is clairvoyance.

89. Fantasy is all the absurd images that are created by a mind filled with aberrations.

90. Instructors must not only give practices to disciples in order to awake the frontal chakra, but they must also teach them how to control the clairvoyance.

91. Clairvoyance is imagination. This chakra resides in the middlebrow.

92. Imagination is translucent. For wise individuals, to imagine is to see.
93. The Age of Reason was initiated by Aristotle. It reached its culmination with Emmanuel Kant and ends now with the birth of the new era of Aquarius.
94. The new era of Aquarius will be the era of the intuitive humanity.
95. We must learn to differentiate between creating an image with the mind and capturing an image that floats in the supra-sensible worlds.
96. Many people may say, "How is it possible for me to capture an image when I am not clairvoyant?"
97. We must answer them that imagination is the same as clairvoyance and that every human being is more or less imaginative, which means, more or less clairvoyant.
98. The most damage that has been caused to the students of esotericism is a result of the false concept that exists about clairvoyance.
99. The creators of this false concept are the 'intellectuals' who have observed the faculties of the imagination with scorn.
100. Wanting to defend themselves from this intellectual disdain, the esotericists began to give a scientific tinge to the imagination and the name of clairvoyance or sixth sense was given to it.
101. This attitude of the esotericists damaged themselves because they remained in confusion.
102. Now, the esotericists (who are victims of the intellectuals) have established a terrible abyss between clairvoyance and imagination.
103. Many people ask themselves, "How can I perceive images without being a clairvoyant?"
104. Poor people! They do not know the treasure which they possess. They ignore that imagination is the same as clairvoyance and that every human being is more or less clairvoyant.

105. The esotericists have wanted to convert the beautiful faculty of clairvoyance into something artificial, technical and difficult.
106. Clairvoyance is imagination. Clairvoyance is the most beautiful, the most simple and pure flower of spirituality.
107. When we re-conquer our lost infancy, all the images that come to our imagination are accompanied by vivid astral colors.
108. The intellectual who despises imagination commits a grave absurdity because everything that exists in nature is a child of imagination.
109. The artist who paints a picture is a great clairvoyant.
110. One remains amazed before Leonardo da Vinci's Christ or before Michelangelo's Madonna.
111. The artist perceives sublime images with his imagination (clairvoyance). He then places them with paint over the canvas or he carves them for his sculpture.
112. Mozart's *Magic Flute* reminds us of an Egyptian initiation...
113. When the mother goddess of the world wants to give a toy to humans for their entertainment, she then places it in the imagination of inventors. This is how we have the radio, the airplane, the automobile, etc.
114. When the tenebrous images of the submerged worlds are captured by the scientists, these are then converted into cannons, machine guns, bombs, etc.
115. Therefore, the entire world is more or less clairvoyant. Imagination cannot be despised because all things are children of imagination.
116. It is necessary to differentiate between the people who have not received any esoteric education and those who have already submitted themselves to great esoteric disciplines.
117. Imagination evolves, develops, and progresses within the igneous rose of the universe.
118. Those who have already caused the magic wheel of their middlebrow to rotate, possess a rich and powerful imag-

ination and all the images which are perceived by them
are accompanied with light, color, heat and sound.

119. We do not deny the existence of clairvoyance.
Clairvoyance is the sixth sense. Its chakra resides in the
middlebrow and has ninety-six rays. What we want is to
increase this concept and to make the student to comprehend that the other name for clairvoyance is imagination. People have forgotten how to use and control divine
clairvoyance. It is necessary for our students to know
that imagination is actually clairvoyance or the sixth
sense situated in the middlebrow.

120. Many people believe that imagination is purely a mental
faculty and that it has nothing to do with the clairvoyant
frontal chakra.

121. This false concept is due to the disdain that intellectuals
feel about imagination, and to the cunning way through
which the esotericists want to make a technicality of this
beautiful faculty of clairvoyance.

122. The frontal chakra of the astral body is intimately related with the frontal chakra of the mental body, with the
frontal chakra of the ethereal body and with the pituitary
gland, situated in the middlebrow of the physical body.

123. Therefore, imagination belongs to all the planes of the
universal consciousness. Clairvoyance is precisely the
same imagination with the susceptibility of development,
evolution and progress within the igneous rose of the
universe.

124. It is necessary for the devotees of the path to have a
well-equilibrated mind.

125. When we speak of logic, we allude to a transcendental
logic that has nothing to do with the text of scholastic
logic.

126. Every internal image has a scientific correspondence in
this plane of physical objectivity.

127. When the images of the student cannot be explained
with a logical concept, it is a sign that the mind of the
student is completely disequilibrated.

128. Every internal image must logically have a satisfactory explanation.
129. There are innumerable amounts of students who have completely unbalanced minds.
130. The Gnostic disciples must cultivate serenity.
131. Serenity is the most powerful key for the development of clairvoyance.
132. Anger destroys the harmony of wholeness and totally damages the petals of the igneous rose of the middle-brow.
133. Anger disarranges the astral light into a poison known as **Imperil** which damages the petals of the igneous rose of the middlebrow and obstructs the channels of the grand sympathetic nervous system. It is necessary to rotate the chakra of the clairvoyance with the vowel "**I**." This vowel must be vocalized daily prolonging the sound of the vowel in the following manner: iiiiiiiiiiiiiii (pronounce the "I" as "ee").
134. We must contemplate internal images within the august serenity of the flames of blazing thought, without the depressing process of reasoning.
135. In the presence of an internal image, our mind must flow integrally with the sweet flow of thought.
136. Our mind vibrates with waves of discernment among the imaginative pictures.
137. Discernment is direct perception of the truth without the process of conceptual selection.
138. When the process of selection divides the mind into the battle of the antitheses, then the internal images are hidden like stars behind the stormy clouds of reasoning.
139. We must learn to think with the heart and to feel with the head.
140. Our mind must become exquisitely sensitive and delicate...
141. The mind must liberate itself from all types of bonds in order to comprehend life, free in its movement.
142. We admire boldness.
143. Desires of all types are bonds for the mind.

144. Prejudice and preconception are bonds for the mind.
145. Schools are cages where the mind remains a prisoner.
146. We must always learn to live in the present, because life is always an eternal instant.
147. Our mind must convert itself into a flexible and delicate instrument for the Innermost.
148. Our mind must convert itself into a child.
149. During the practices of internal meditation, we must be in the most absolute interior repose, because every agitation of the mind and every attitude or impatience disturbs the mind and impedes the perception of internal images.
150. In the physical world, every activity is accompanied by the movement of our hands, legs, etc. However, in the internal worlds, we need the most profound internal repose and absolute calmness in order to receive the internal images that come to the mind like a grace... like a blessing.
151. It is indispensable that our disciples cultivate the beautiful quality of veneration.
152. We must profoundly venerate all sacred and divine things.
153. We must profoundly venerate all the works of the Creator.
154. We must profoundly venerate the venerable masters of the Universal White Fraternity.
155. Respect and veneration completely open the doors of the superior worlds for us.
156. We must not have preferences for anyone. We must attend the beggar and the gentleman with the same respect and veneration.
157. We must cultivate the same courtesy for the rich and the poor and for the aristocrat and the peasant in order to equally attend to them without any preferences.
158. We must cultivate patience and prudence.
159. The ants and the bees are patient and prudent.
160. We must end all eagerness for accumulation and for greed.

161. We must learn to be indifferent before gold and wealth.
162. We must learn to appreciate the Doctrine of the Heart more.
163. He who despises the Doctrine of the Heart because he follows the Doctrine of the Eye (theories, schools, bookish culture, etc.) can never reach great realizations.
164. We must learn how to know good from evil and evil from good.
165. In everything that is evil, there is something good; in everything that is good, there is something evil.
166. Although it seems incredible, the Mary Magdalenes are much closer to initiation than many innocent girls.
167. Although it seems unusual to the student, the one who is pointed at and accused with the finger is often closer to the initiation than the hypocritical, sanctimonious one who sweetly smiles before the people in the auditorium of the lodge or temple.
168. Paul of Tarsus was an executioner and an assassin before the event that took place in his journey to Damascus.
169. The instantaneous transformation of this man surprised all the saints of Jerusalem.
170. The evil one converted himself into a prophet...
171. This is the mystery of Baphomet.
172. Animal pedestals sustain the sacred objects of the temples. The legs of the thrones of the masters are made of monsters.
173. Christ knew how to appreciate the beauty of the teeth on a decomposing body of a dog.
174. Blue flames were blazing in the demon Beelzebub. These flames assisted him in order to transform him into a disciple of the White Hierarchy.
175. Crime is often hidden within the incense of prayer.
176. The disciple must not judge anyone, nor criticize anyone, in order to form a rich interior life.
177. At times, it is a crime to speak, and at other times, it is a crime to be silent.
178. It is a crime to speak when we must be silent, and likewise, it is a crime to be silent when we must speak.

179. There is the need to learn how to control the word and to know how to calculate with exactness the result of our words.
180. One word can serve as a blessing to one person, yet as an insult to another.
181. Therefore, we must calculate very well the result of a word before it is uttered.
182. The lords of karma judge the results of actions without taking into account good intentions.
183. Our mind must be simple and humble and filled with the most profound respect.
184. Our disciples must carefully avoid any argument in order not to waste their energy uselessly.
185. Whosoever wants to accept the doctrine of the Gnostics, let him accept it. Whosoever does not want to accept it is not yet mature. Therefore, it is useless to form an argument in order to convince such an individual.
186. *"May argument be forbidden. May discord in words be thrown down. May all weeds leave the path clear."*
187. We must cultivate gratitude because ingratitude and treason are joined.
188. It is necessary to eliminate envy, because the Judas's who sell the master for thirty silver coins are the outcome of envy.
189. Envy is a poisonous flower that is greatly abundant among the tenebrous swamps of all the spiritual schools of the world.
190. Envy is often disguised with the cloak of the judge.
191. We must cultivate sincerity, because the most beautiful flowers of the spirit sprout within the substance of sincerity.
192. All these qualities will give us a rich interior life. This is how we internally prepare ourselves for the great esoteric disciplines of the mind, that blaze within the burning flames of the universe.

Chapter 18

The Arhat's Cross

1. The fire of your igneous rose, which is situated in the larynx of your mental body, burns and sparkles within the ardent flames of the universe.
2. Now, oh arhat, you enter the three higher chambers of the tower of your temple.
3. The Kundalini of your mental body opens the first chamber of your cerebellum.
4. Do you know what this signifies, my child?
5. Woe to you, oh arhat!
6. Receive your fourth cross, so that you may crucify your mental body.
7. Do you know what this signifies, sibling of mine?
8. Do you know what the mind signifies?
9. You are now worthy of pity, oh arhat!
10. You must work in the great work of the Father.
11. You will be an immolated lamb upon the altar of sacrifice.
12. You will work incessantly for humanity.
13. You will perform works of genius, but do not expect a crown of laurels, my child...
14. Remember that you must sacrifice your mind...
15. Humanity will make a mockery of your work. They will ridicule you and give you bile to drink...
16. Your works of merit will be received with loud guffaws, and humanity will reward all of your sacrifices with their deepest despise.
17. You are worthy of compassion, oh arhat!
18. The cross of your mental body is large and very heavy.
19. Your enemies will be your very spiritual brothers and sisters.
20. They will punish you severely and they will mock you, oh arhat!

21. The spiritual devotees of all the denominations will qualify you as an evil one, and they will ridicule you, oh arhat!

22. You will be slandered, mocked and hated by all the world. This is how you will crucify your mind, oh arhat!

23. Apollonius of Tyana spent his last years enclosed within a prison. Paracelsus was qualified as a friend of gypsies and executioners by all of his "Judas's." All the pedants of that time hated to death the eminent Theophrastus Bombastus of Hohenheim (Aureola Paracelsus).

24. This great wise man (Paracelsus) gave humanity medical wisdom that will be accepted and comprehended only by the human species of the Aquarian Age.

25. Agrippa, hated by men, wandered from city to city, and all the world distrusted him and qualified him as a sorcerer.

26. All the saints of Jerusalem, all the martyrs of humanity, were hated and persecuted.

27. Oh arhat, the cross of your mental body is heavy!

28. You are now an enigmatic personage, my child, and all the spiritual brothers qualify you as an evil one, as being intolerant, as tenebrous, simply because they do not comprehend you. You know this.

29. Blessed be those who love us, because they comprehend us; blessed be those who hate us, because they do not comprehend us.

Chapter 19
The Woman

1. Woman has the same rights as man.
2. Woman also reaches the level of adept of the White Fraternity.
3. Joan of Arc is a master of Major Mysteries of the White Fraternity.
4. H.P. Blavatsky, author of *The Secret Doctrine*, reached the level of adept and she is a master of Major Mysteries of the White Fraternity.
5. In almost all the temples of the mysteries, we find many female adepts working for humanity.
6. Woman awakens her sacred serpent in the same way as man.
7. If a woman who is married wants to awaken her Kundalini, then she must practice sexual magic with her husband.
8. Married women must transmute by means of the mind, as we have taught in the preceding pages.
9. Sexual alchemy is the fundamental base of all progress.
10. Sexual alchemy is the foundation of the wisdom of the fire.
11. The temple, the womb and the "matrass" of the sexual laboratory is love.
12. The Philosophical Stone of the alchemist is elaborated when combining salt, sulphur and mercury within this matrass of sexual alchemy, by means of a progressive erotic combustion.
13. Within the sexual matrass of our organic laboratory, the explosions of passionate fire combine certain ethereal, astral, mental, volitive, conscious, and divine arcana. This occurs in order to elaborate certain igneous elements, whose substantial principles belong to the Innermost, with the ardent fire of the erotic thirst.
14. The woman accumulates a very large quantity of elemental fire from nature while in the state of sexual excite-

ment, and when her fire is combined with the erotic magnetism of her husband, then it engenders certain cosmic powers whose tremendous explosions open the spinal chambers.

15. The boiling passionate fires of man and woman, when mutually and erotically combined, create truly ardent tempests that disturb the atmosphere and cause the tenebrous ones, who are the escorts of each chamber, to go mad.

16. These submerged entities attack the intrepid ones by defending the fires, whose synthetic and scientific principles are enclosed in the thirty-three internal chambers of our spinal column.

17. These tenebrous ones defend their rights, and for this reason they qualify us as thieves of powers.

18. This is the mystery of Baphomet. The rose elaborates its perfume with the clay of the earth. The slithering worm does not like the gardener who removes its clay. Our disciples will now comprehend on what basis do the tenebrous ones qualify the sexual alchemists as thieves.

19. Each chamber is strongly defended by tenebrous legions. It is necessary to defeat these tenebrous ones with the edge of the sword in order to take each chamber by force.

20. Now the devotees of the path will understand why Christ said that heaven is taken by force.

21. The twelve zodiacal salts ardently boil within our endocrine glands during the moments of sexual alchemy.

22. These twelve zodiacal salts enclose the seminal principles of the twelve constellations, whose ardent powers act over these tiny laboratories (which are our endocrine glands) in particular by activating the hormonal production of our liquid nervous system.

23. The super-excitement of our endocrine glands is accompanied by gigantic igneous combinations within all of the chakras and essences of our internal vehicles.

24. When sexually excited, the woman has the power to transplant the synthetic principles of the twelve salts to the larynx of the man. This is how such an organ

acquires hermaphrodite principles that later give the Innermost the power to create by means of the word.

25. The combination of the igneous principles between the man and the woman are also intimately related with a sequence of salty interchanges that prepare the feminine larynx as an angelic creative organ.

26. The very ardent fire of great sexual excitement gives origin to gigantic combinations of principles, whose synthetic outcome becomes the opening of the spinal chambers.

27. The stronger the restraint of the act is, and the more violent the fight is, the more potent will be the seminal steam that rises. Thus, the force of the ascension of the Kundalini will be more terrific.

28. The key of sexual dominion resides in the mind.

29. The mind is dominated by means of willpower.

30. We must flagellate the mind with the terrific whip of willpower when restraining passionate excitement, because the den of desire resides in the mind.

31. We must speak to the mind as this, "Mind, take this sexual excitement away from me immediately."

32. This formula permits us to take away the intense passion in the precise moment of the restraint of the act.

33. The union with the Innermost is possible only by means of sexual alchemy.

34. If we take the mental body of a theorizing pseudo-spiritual student, and very carefully examine it, we find that it is a true walking library.

35. If we then carefully examine the church of the coccyx, or the chakra Muladhara, we then find that the Kundalini is totally enclosed there without showing the slightest signs of awakening. If we examine the Shushumna channel of this theorizing student, we then find not even a trace of the sacred fire. We find that the thirty-three chambers of this student are totally filled with darkness.

36. This internal examination will bring us to the conclusion that such a student is lamentably wasting his time.

37. The sacred fire awakens when the lunar and solar atoms of our seminal system come into contact within the bone of the coccyx.

38. However, if we waste our solar atoms with the seminal ejaculation, then there is not a sufficient amount of atoms to make contact in order to awaken this fire.

39. The student can have a mental body converted into a true library, but all of the thirty-three chambers of his spinal column will be disconnected, in complete and profound darkness.

40. In conclusion, this student is an inhabitant of the darkness, of the abyss.

41. It is impossible to raise the fire of Kundalini with only the lunar atoms of the cephalous rachidial liquid.

42. It is indispensable that the solar atoms of the seminal system make contact with the lunar atoms of the cephalous rachidial liquid in order to awaken the sacred fire.

43. If we waste the solar atoms, we will then have no capital in order to make an atomic combination, which permits the awakening of the Kundalini by means of sexual magic.

44. The Kundalini is of an absolutely sexual nature and it is only possible to awaken it by means of sexual alchemy.

45. If we carefully examine the internal constitution of a mystical person, we will find a very beautiful conscious body (Buddhic) and the luminous and reflective ethers of the ethereal body will be very voluminous. However, the common and current mystic ejaculates his seminal liquid, and when the chakra Muladhara is analyzed, we find that the Kundalini is entwined there, without showing any signs of awakening.

46. The thirty-three chambers of the spinal column of this mystic of our example are filled with darkness, because the fire has never passed through them.

47. Good philanthropic deeds beautify the luminous and reflective ethers of this mystic and his bookish culture gives to his mind a rich erudition. Yet, this mystic has not penetrated into the mysteries of the fire because

his Kundalini is not awakened. In spite of the fact that he may be a good and virtuous person, he will not go beyond being a good and virtuous person. He will not go beyond being a good and kind shadow within the cold and the darkness of the abyss.

48. Some people sustain that the Kundalini can be awakened by means of yoga.

49. We do not deny this affirmation.

50. However, we affirm that the authentic yogi is totally chaste.

51. If this is not so, then yogis would not have atomic capital in order to awaken the Kundalini.

52. Vivekananda says in his lectures of Raja Yoga that the yogi must be totally chaste in order to convert his sexual force into ojas (Christic energy).

53. This is how yogis achieve the awakening of the Kundalini and the union with the Innermost.

54. The sexual alchemy of yogis is related with respiratory exercises and with certain practices of internal meditation that have never been printed in any published book.

55. If the yogi fornicates, he does not have sufficient atomic capital in order to make the spinal fires ascend. The yogi lamentably wastes his time.

56. Yoga practices are only for those that belong to the Asian ray.

57. Among the Gnostics, the woman is the priestess of the blessed mother goddess of world.

58. There are some who want to reach the union with the Innermost without even taking the Kundalini into account.

59. These students are perfectly lost, because the union with the Innermost is possible only by means of fire. This is why the word INRI (Ignis Natura Renovatur Integra) was placed upon the cross of the martyr of Calvary. The fire renews nature incessantly.

60. Are you a Gnostic? Are you a mystic? Are you a yogi?

61. Remember, good disciple, you can only enter Eden through the door from which you departed. That door is sex.

62. It is said that there are many ways. We, the masters of the Major Mysteries of the great White Lodge affirm that there is only one door to enter into Eden, and that door is sex.

63. All who do not obey the command of the Lord Jehovah, all who continue to eat the forbidden fruit, are disciples of the doctrine of the Baalim. As the sacred scriptures state, for them will be the burning lake of fire and sulphur. This is the Second Death.

64. The Gnostic man must intensely love his priestess...

65. Woman must live always filled with harmony, and she must cultivate the artistic sense.

66. Woman penetrates the distinct halls of the fire and she Christifies herself at the same time as the sacred fire ascends through her spinal medulla.

67. Woman must restrain the sexual act and withdraw from the man before the orgasm in order to avoid the loss of her seminal liquid.

68. This is how the Kundalini awakens in the woman, just as it does in the man.

69. Masculine magnetism, when mixed with feminine magnetism, starts the awakening of the sacred fires in woman.

70. Woman must cultivate beauty, music, and love.

71. Let us awake within ourselves the esoteric majesty of our interior beauty.

72. Allow me to affirm the majesty of our Being:

73. "I am"[9] a solitary tree. "I am" the Tree of Life.

---

9   "Only Christ can say, "I am the way, the truth and the life. I am the light. I am the life. I am the good shepherd. I am the bread. I am the resurrection." The Being is the one who receives the Being of his Being, the "I Am," who is (in each one of us) a breath of the great breath, our particular Ray, that is Him, Him, Him. The "I AM" is the Internal Christ of each human being, our divine "Augoides," the Logos. Whosoever receives the Crown of Life has the right to say, "I am Him, I am Him, I am Him." - Tarot and Kabbalah

Chapter 20
The Lion of the Law

1. You have now entered the thirty-second vertebra of your mental body's spinal medulla, oh arhat!
2. This is the second holy chamber of your head.
3. The burning fire of the universe now ardently sparks in this holy chamber of your mental body.
4. This is the degree of the lion of the law.
5. Naturae Santa Sororera has given birth to a new lion of the law in the world of the cosmic mind.
6. Examine well the hoof of your beast and be happy, oh arhat!
7. A terrific ray and a frightful exhalation falls from the infinite heavens, and with the thunder of their voices makes the earth tremble...
8. It is the ray of cosmic justice.
9. This ray is beyond good and evil.
10. The lion of the law is beyond good and evil.
11. The lion of the law knows good from evil and evil from good. In everything good there is something evil, and in everything evil there is something good.
12. The super-human is beyond good and evil.
13. Justice is the supreme mercy and the supreme severity of the law.
14. The intelligence of the super-human is frightening, but the super-human scorns intelligence because intelligence is a quality of Prakriti and Prana (matter and energy).
15. The Innermost is beyond intelligence. He abides in the kingdom of supreme omniscience.
16. The Innermost is even far beyond love. He abides in the supreme kingdom of happiness.
17. On an inferior plane, the happiness of God expresses itself as love, and love is the perfection of wisdom.
18. The two columns of our White Fraternity are wisdom and love.

19. The scale of cosmic justice has two plates in perfect equilibrium.
20. Wisdom is in one of the two plates and love is in the other.
21. Love and wisdom maintain the two plates of the scale in perfect equilibrium.
22. Any disequilibrium of the scale is punished by the lions of the law.
23. Children of humans, remember that the two plates of the cosmic scale are wisdom and love.
24. Have you sinned against the goddess moon? If so, how can you demand happiness in love?
25. Have you sinned against wisdom? Then, sibling of mine, how can you be surrounded with happiness?
26. The lion of the law is fought with the scale. When an inferior law is transcended by a superior law, the superior law washes away the inferior law. Perform good deeds so that you may pay your debts.
27. Whosoever has capital, pays and does well in business. When we do not have capital and a fault is found in the books of karma, we must pay with pain.
28. Now enter, oh arhat, into the holy temple of the cosmic mind in order to receive your feast.
29. You are now a new lion of the law in the world of the cosmic mind.
30. Your mind burns within the ardent sparks of Naturae Santa Sororera.
31. The mind of the lions of cosmic mind burns within the blazing flames of this igneous rose of the universe.
32. "Love is law, but conscious love."

Chapter 21
Jezebel's Table

1. *"Notwithstanding I have a few things against thee, because thou*
    sufferest that woman Jezebel, which calleth herself a prophetess,
    to teach and to seduce my servants to commit fornication, and to
    eat things sacrificed unto idols.

    "And I gave her space to repent of her
    fornication; and she repented not.

    "Behold, I will cast her into a bed, and them that
    commit adultery with her into great tribulation,
    except they repent of their deeds.

    "And I will kill her children with death; and all the
    churches shall know that I am he which searcheth the
    reins and hearts: and I will give unto every one of you
    according to your works." —Revelation 2:20-23

2. The prophets of Baalim eat at Jezebel's table (the Baalim
    are the black magicians).

3. The prophets of Baalim who teach how to "mystically"
    fornicate and how to eat things sacrificed unto idols
    are all the theorists and spiritual devotees of the world.
    Therefore, all their teachings are food sacrificed unto
    idols.

4. The gentleman Parsival Krumm-Heller, sovereign com-
    mander of the "so-called" Ancient Rosicrucian Order,
    with headquarters in Germany, is sending courses of
    black sexual magic to his tenebrous disciples. In his
    course, he advises the "mystical" seminal ejaculation
    (orgasm).

5. This is how Jezebel seduced my servants. This is how she
    teaches them to fornicate and how to eat theories sacri-
    ficed unto idols.

6. This course of negative and tenebrous sexual magic is the
    same horrible and satanic tantric doctrine preached and

taught by all the prophets of Baalim who eat at Jezebel's table.

7. With this repugnant phallic cult, the Kundalini awakens negatively, and gloomily submerges itself into the human's own atomic infernos, giving the astral body the horrible and satanic appearance of the Lucifers.

8. The gentleman Parsival Krumm-Heller betrayed his own father (Arnold Krumm-Heller) with his tenebrous phallic cult. He publicly remained declared as a black magician.

9. *"And the Lord Jehovah commanded the man, saying, Of every tree of the garden thou mayest freely eat: But of the tree of the knowledge of good and evil, thou shalt not eat of it, for in the day that thou eatest thereof thou shalt surely die."* –Genesis 2:16-17

10. These are the commands of the Lord Jehovah. Everyone who violates these commands is a black magician.

11. These are the commands of the Lord Jehovah. Everyone who violates these commands will be cast into the burning lake of fire and sulphur. This is the second death.

12. The second death is a psychic death. The tantric personality of the fornicator is separated from his divine triad and is submerged into a state of demonic consciousness. Then, he is submerged into the atomic worlds, known in the Orient as Avitchi...

13. These tantric personalities are then slowly disintegrated, separated from their superior being.

14. *"And I will kill her children with death; and all the churches shall know that I am he which searcheth the reins and hearts and I will give unto every one of you according to your works."*

15. The prophets of Baalim who eat at Jezebel's table will die in the abyss.
Listen to me, sibling of mine: *"Thus saith Jehovah of the hosts; If thou wilt walk in my ways, and if thou wilt keep my charge, then thou shalt also judge my house, and shalt also keep my courts, and I will give thee places to walk among these that stand by."* –Zachariah 3:7

16. Sibling of mine, keep the command of the Lord Jehovah. See the forbidden fruit. Be nourished with its aroma. Be delighted with its perfume, but do not eat it, because the

burning lake of fire and sulphur is for fornicators. This is the second death.

17. Trillions of solar atoms are lost in the seminal ejaculation (orgasm). Afterwards, in order to replace them, our sexual organs collect trillions of satanic atoms from the infernos of the human being. These satanic atoms are absorbed within the astral body and give it the appearance of Satan.

18. The negative theory of the tenebrous ones consists of taking advantage of the absorbed hormones in order to awaken the Kundalini and to achieve tantric powers.

19. Nevertheless, what awakens with this practice is the negative aspect of the serpent (Kundabuffer). When submerged into the human being's own atomic infernos, this negative aspect of the serpent assumes the tantric form in the astral body, which is represented by the tail of Satan.

20. The sexual glands are not closed capsules. They excrete hormones and they also absorb hormones.

21. The prophets of the Baalim who eat at Jezebel's table take advantage of the hormones of sexual absorption by means of their phallic cult. This is done in order to awaken their satanic powers. In this manner, the woman Jezebel, who calls herself a prophetess, teaches and seduces my servants to commit fornication, and to eat of things sacrificed unto idols.

22. *"And I gave her space to repent of her fornication; and she repented not. Behold I will cast her into a bed, and them that commit adultery with her into great tribulation, except they repent of their deeds."* —Revelation 2:21-22

23. The mind of our disciples must be liberated from the satanic fires.

24. The tenebrous Luzbel, dweller of the Avitchi, carries an ancient scroll on his tantric tail (Kundabuffer), on which this negative sexual magic is written with ominous characters. This is what the traitor Parsival Krumm-Heller and the sinister Baal Omar Cherenzi-Lind are teaching.

25. There is the need to transmute the water into wine in order to raise our metallic serpent upon the reed, as Moses did in the wilderness.
26. This is how the soul unites itself with the Innermost, within the blazing, universal flames.
27. The mind must become chaste and pure within the august thunder of thought.
28. The mind must not eat things sacrificed unto idols.
29. The mind must not let itself be seduced by Jezebel.
30. Be pure, sibling of mine, be perfect and be chaste in thought, word and action.
31. This path is very difficult, so straight and so narrow, and it is because no one likes chastity.
32. The spiritual devotees of all schools hate chastity because it is the door to Eden. They do not like Eden because they eat at Jezebel's table and they worship the Baalim.
33. *"Strive to enter in at the strait gate: for many, I say unto you, will seek to enter in, and shall not be able.*

    "When once the master of the house is risen up, and hath shut to the door, and ye begin to stand without, and to knock at the door, saying, Lord, Lord, open unto us; and he shall answer and say unto you, I know you not whence ye are;

    "Then shall ye begin to say We have eaten and drunk in thy presence, and thou hast taught in our streets.

    "But ye shall say, I tell you, I know you not whence ye are; depart from me workers of iniquity.

    "There shall be weeping and gnashing of teeth, when ye shall see ABRAHAM, and ISAAC, and JACOB, and all the prophets, in the Kingdom of GOD, and you yourselves thrust out." —Luke 13:24-28
34. Humanity has been fornicating for more than eighteen million years, and if the way of fornication was the positive way, then humanity would not have hunger, there would be no wars, and all human beings would now be angels.

35. But, behold humanity, sibling of mine, it has been ejaculating the semen for eighteen million years. Is it perhaps happy? Have humans now become angels? Is earth an Eden?

36. If the way of animal passion was the true way, then the human being would now be an angel.

37. What is new in the teachings of Parsival and Cherenzi?

38. Is it perhaps a new thing to teach human beings how to ejaculate the semen?

39. In which epoch did the human being become converted into an angel by fornication?

40. Human evolution has failed, precisely because of the seminal ejaculation (orgasm). Now what?

41. There was a great reunion of mahatmas in a temple of Asian Tibet, at which all of the great creators of the human being were present.

42. A great son of the fire descended from the infinite space and spoke the following:

43. "My brothers and sisters, we must recognize that human evolution has failed. We, the gods, committed a mistake when creating this humanity. There, in the dawn of life, we wanted to convert these virginal sparks into gods, but the result was demons."

44. Following this, the great being was enumerating, one by one, all of the prophets who had been sent to help humanity. He was narrating how all of them were stoned, persecuted, poisoned, and crucified by the human species.

45. Upon finishing his discourse, the great son of the light departed from the temple.

46. The major brothers and sisters then consulted the god Sirius in order to try to resolve this gigantic problem.

47. The answer arrived swiftly. It can be synthesized in the following verses:

"And he cried mightily with a strong voice, saying, Babylon the great is fallen, is fallen, and is become the habitation of devils, and the hold of every foul spirit, and a cage of every unclean and hateful bird. For all nations have drunk of the wine of the wrath

of her fornication, and the kings of the earth have committed fornication with her, and the merchants of the earth are waxed rich through the abundance of her delicacies." —Revelation 18:2-3

48. Only a tiny handful of souls will reincarnate in the new Aquarian Age.

49. Millions of human souls, separated from the Innermost, are now sinking into the tenebrous abyss and they will not reincarnate during the new Aquarian Age.

50. *"And the great harlot is dressed with the colors purple and scarlet, she is decked with gold, precious stones and pearls, and her chalice is filled with abomination, filthiness and fornication."*

51. This is Jezebel, at whose table the prophets of Baalim eat. The dogs shall eat Jezebel by the wall of Jezreel.

52. Upon the head of Jezebel, she that calls herself a prophetess, is written this name: "Mystery, Babylon the great, the mother of fornications and abominations of the earth."

Chapter 22

The Crown Chakra

1. You have reached the thirty-third chamber, oh arhat! The higher three chambers of your head have now been united by means of fire.
2. A metallic bell makes all the places of the earth tremble, and the crown center of your pineal gland shines within the blazing flames of the cosmic mind.
3. Your white tunic shines terrifically within the ardent sparks of the universal flames.
4. Ineffable orchestras resound in the temple within the great rhythms of the fire.
5. This igneous rose of your mental crown makes your face and your august temples shine within the undulating flames of the mental world.
6. This is the lotus of one thousand petals. This is the crown of saints. This is the eye of polyvoyance. This is the Diamond Eye.
7. Oh arhat! You must now connect your pineal gland with your pituitary gland by means of the fire.
8. Persevere and do not lose heart, my child. Throw your crown at the feet of the Lamb.
9. You have received the crown of life, oh arhat!
10. You have previously performed this work with the igneous serpent of your physical body, with the igneous serpent of your ethereal body, and with the igneous serpent of your astral body.
11. Now, sibling of mine, you have performed this work with the serpent of your mental body. This is the fourth degree of the power of the fire.
12. Later, you must perform an identical work with the fifth, sixth, and seventh serpents.
13. There are two groups of serpents. Each group has three serpents, plus the sublime coronation of the seventh serpent that unites us with the one, with the law, and with the Father.

14. Therefore, we must pass our thirty-three chambers seven times.

15. The seven degrees of the power of the fire are scaled in a spiral way.

16. Ezekiel described the seven degrees of the power of the fire and the thirty-three chambers of our temple as follows:

17. *"And the side chambers were three, one over another, and thirty in order; and they entered into the wall which was of the house for the side chambers round about, that they might have hold, but they had not hold in the wall of the house.*

    "And there was an enlarging, and a winding about still upward to the side chambers: for the winding about of the house went still upward round about the house: therefore the breadth of the house was still upward, and so increased from the lowest chamber to the highest by the midst.

    "I saw also the height of the house round about: the foundations of the side chambers were a full reed of six great cubits." —Ezekiel 41:6-8

18. *"Then said he unto me, The north chambers and the south chambers, which are before the separate place, they be holy chambers, where the priests that approach unto the Lord shall eat the most holy things: there shall they lay the most holy things, and the meat offering, and the sin offering, and the trespass offering; for the place is holy.*

    "When the priests enter therein, then shall they not go out of the holy place into the outer court, but there they shall lay their garments wherein they minister, for they are holy, and shall put on other garments, and shall approach to those things which are for the people." —Ezekiel 42:13-14

19. Each of the thirty-three vertebrae of our spinal column has an atomic god of immaculate beauty.

20. Now, within the mind of the arhat all thirty-three atomic gods flamingly shine.

21. The seven igneous roses of the spinal medulla ardently spark with the burning fire of your medullar channel, oh arhat!

Chapter 23

The Seven Igneous Roses of the Reed

1. Our spinal column has seven igneous roses.
2. With the sacred fire of the Shushumna channel these seven igneous roses enter into activity.
3. This sacred fire is engendered when the solar and lunar atoms of our two ganglionic cords come into contact.
4. In the East, these two sympathetic cords are known as Ida and Pingala.
5. Ida and Pingala function along the curved surface of our spinal medulla, where the Shushumna channel is located.
6. These two sympathetic cords are our two witnesses, our two olive branches, and the two candlesticks that are before the god of the earth.
7. These two cords emerge from the center of the sacrum, which is called the Triveni of the medulla oblongata.
8. When the solar and lunar atoms of these two cords come into contact in the sacrum, the sacred fire awakens, and the Triveni or Muladhara enters into activity. This is the church of the coccyx which has the power of opening the prostatic or fundamental chakra.
9. The vertebral column is known by the Hindus as Brahmadanda or the staff of Brahma. It is also symbolized by the bamboo reed with seven knots that the yogis from India carry.
10. The Shushumna channel together with the two sympathetic cords are symbolized by the bamboo reed with three knots, that the Trans-himalayan yogis use. They continuously reunite at Lake Manasarovar. This is why they are known as Tridandins[10]. This is what the Brahmanic thread[11] of the three vital airs of pure Akasha symbolizes.

---

10   "...he who has been initiated into three degrees, who carries the three rods, and who has power over three things: thought, speech, and action." - Louis Jacolliot, Occult Science in India

11   The "sacred thread" (Sanskrit yajñopavitam or upavita) is a thin cord composed of three cotton strands.

11. The right ganglionic cord corresponds to the right nasal cavity. The left ganglionic cord belongs to the left nasal cavity.
12. The right ganglionic cord is solar, positive. The left ganglionic cord is lunar, negative.
13. When the solar and lunar atoms of the Brahmanic cord come into contact in the center of the sacrum Triveni, then the Kundalini enters into activity. It then opens its way towards Brahmarandra, which is the frontal fontanel of a newborn, in order to shine brightly in the middle-brow, neck, and heart, in successive order.
14. The seat of Brahma is in the heart. The heart is the seat of Atman-Buddhi-Manas. The spiritual man resides in the heart.
15. The first serpent, that corresponds to the physical body, reaches only to Brahmarandra, in order to shine with splendor in the frontal chakra. This center has ninety-six rays.
16. The second serpent, that corresponds to the ethereal body, reaches only to the middlebrow.
17. However, the five other serpents must inevitably reach the heart.
18. The second rose of our spinal column opens the solar plexus. This center has ten rays: five active and five passive.
19. However, the sacred fire puts all of them into complete activity.
20. The brain and the heart totally shine with the fire of Kundalini.
21. The septenary activity of the sacred fire in the pineal gland is reflected in the aura of the heart. This is how the sacred fire places the seven cardiac centers into activity.
22. The third center enters into complete activity when the Kundalini lights the third igneous rose.
23. The chakra of the heart has twelve petals.
24. The fourth igneous rose opens our igneous wings and is intimately related with the sense of touch.

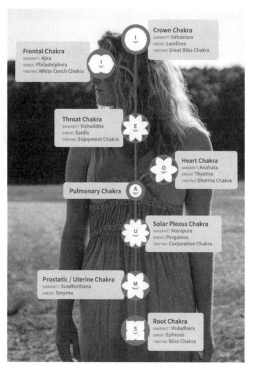

Frontal Chakra
SANSKRIT: Ajna
GREEK: Philadelpheia
TIBETAN: White Conch Chakra

Crown Chakra
SANSKRIT: Sahasrara
GREEK: Laodicea
TIBETAN: Great Bliss Chakra

Throat Chakra
SANSKRIT: Vishuddha
GREEK: Sardis
TIBETAN: Enjoyment Chakra

Heart Chakra
SANSKRIT: Anahata
GREEK: Thyatira
TIBETAN: Dharma Chakra

Pulmonary Chakra

Solar Plexus Chakra
SANSKRIT: Manipura
GREEK: Pergamos
TIBETAN: Conjuration Chakra

Prostatic / Uterine Chakra
SANSKRIT: Svadhisthana
GREEK: Smyrna

Root Chakra
SANSKRIT: Muladhara
GREEK: Ephesus
TIBETAN: Bliss Chakra

CHAKRAS

25. The fifth igneous rose opens our chakra of the thyroid, which is related with the esoteric ear.
26. The sixth igneous rose belongs to the thirty-second vertebra of our spinal column. This is the second highest chamber of the head, and it opens the frontal chakra that gives us clairvoyance.
27. This center has ninety-six rays and it shines in the middlebrow with the sacred fire.
28. The frontal chakra is the organ of vision in the psychic plane.
29. This organ resides in the pituitary gland, which has seven types of hormones.
30. The seventh igneous rose corresponds to the pineal gland.
31. The pituitary gland is only the instrument or the carrier of the light of the pineal gland.

32. In the woman, the pineal gland corresponds to the uterus and its peduncles with the fallopian tubes.

33. In the man, the pineal gland is found intimately related with the sexual glands.

34. We now explain to ourselves why this chakra cannot enter into activity in fornicators.

35. Any sexual decline is reflected in the pineal gland.

36. The entire majesty of God is expressed in the seventh igneous rose.

37. This seventh igneous rose is the crown of the saints, and it has one thousand petals of indescribable splendor.

38. Our brain has seven cavities, and our heart also has seven centers.

39. These seven cavities of our brain correspond to the seven scales of the divine harmonies and are occupied by pure Akasha...

40. The psychic-mental man resides in the head with his seven gates, and Atman-Buddhi-Manas (the heavenly man) resides in the heart.

41. We must unite the mind with the heart by means of the fire.

42. The chalice and the heart must march in complete equilibrium. This is possible only by uniting the head and the heart by means of the fire.

43. The brain's circumvolutions have been formed by the argentine armor of the mental body.

44. The third ventricle of the brain is filled with light and this light becomes splendorous with the sacred fire of the Kundalini.

45. The sixth cavity belongs to the pineal gland.

46. The pineal gland or crown center is a rounded body of six to eight millimetres in length. It possesses a reddish-grey, obscure color and is connected with the posterior part of the third ventricle of the brain.

47. It has two very fine and beautiful medullar fibers in its base, that diversely direct themselves towards the optic thalamus.

48. The pituitary body is found connected to the pineal gland by a very fine capillary channel, which disappears in the corpse.
49. The pineal gland is surrounded by a very fine and tiny sand.
50. This tiny sand is the "Acerbulus Cerebri," the concreteness of the mental body and the efficient instrument of the mind.
51. The seven capital chakras that govern the seven plexes reside in the head.
52. When the mental body has been totally Christified by the fourth serpent, it converts itself into an efficient instrument for the Innermost.
53. The real Being utilizes the mind as an element of regulation and control for the seven astral plexes.
54. The mind controls its plexes by means of the seven capital chakras of the brain.
55. The solar plexus is our brain of emotions and when entering into activity it awakens the hepatic and splenic plexes.
56. The heart represents our divine triad[12]. The hepatic and splenic plexes represent our inferior quaternary[13]. Esoterically, the solar plexus is the brain of the stomach in which we place Saturn, which is the sun of our organism.
57. The spiritual devotees of all schools have studied the astral chakras, but they have never studied the seven candlesticks of the mental body that glow in the fire of the arhat.
58. Our chakras are septuple in their constitution, as well as in our sacred serpent and our Brahmanic cord.
59. The seven igneous roses of our spinal medulla are also septuple in their internal constitution.
60. Our brain has seven cavities and our heart also has seven divine centers.

12   The sephiroth Chesed, Geburah, Tiphereth. See illustration on page 8.
13   The sephiroth Netzach, Hod, Yesod, Malkuth.

61. The sacred fire enters into activity when the solar and lunar atoms of the Brahmanic cord come into contact in the Triveni. This contact is possible only by intensely practicing sexual magic with our spouse, or by means of the sacrifice of a complete and definitive sexual abstention.

62. The most powerful mantras that are known in the entire infinite for the awakening of the sacred fire are: **Kandil Bandil Rrrrrr**.

63. These mantras are vocalized in a singing form as follows: KAN (resounding voice) DIL (decreasing voice) BAN (resounding voice) DIL (decreasing voice) Rrrrrrr (rolled). The letter 'R' is pronounced with a high sound and rolled, imitating the sound of the rattles of a rattlesnake.

64. The first igneous rose of our spinal column corresponds to the reproductive and respiratory organs of the race.

65. The second igneous rose corresponds to the sense of taste. The third igneous rose corresponds to the heart. The fourth igneous rose corresponds to the wings. The fifth igneous rose corresponds to the ear. The sixth igneous rose corresponds to the sense of sight. The seventh igneous rose corresponds to the Diamond Eye, Eye of Brahma, crown chakra or center of polyvoyance that permits us to see in all the planes of consciousness.

66. All of our senses are intimately related with the tattvas and with the distinct spheres or planes of cosmic consciousness that express themselves through the seven igneous roses of our spinal column.

67. The awakening of the seven igneous roses gives us access to the superlative planes of cosmic consciousness.

68. This ascension is performed in a spiral through the seven degrees of the power of the fire.

69. The sacred fire opens the avenues of the truth.

70. The sense of touch belongs to the fourth igneous rose, to the eternal wings that permit us to soar from sphere to sphere in the planes of superlative consciousness, where only the happiness of the Being reigns.

Chapter 24

The Reed of Your Mental Body

1. The serpent of your mental body has now reached Brahmarandra, the sacred center of the frontal fontanel of newborn children.
2. This is the superior orifice of your reed, oh arhat!
3. This orifice remains closed in the common and current persons, yet the master opens it with the fire.
4. Receive the symbolic reed of your mental body, oh arhat!
5. The sacred fire has opened its way through your cranium, and now departs, and enters into the surrounding atmosphere like a blaze of flames that ardently spark.
6. You shine in the world of the mind as a splendorous sun, oh arhat!
7. You have converted yourself into an ardent flame in the world of the cosmic mind.
8. Ineffable music resounds in the environs of the temple. Receive your bouquet of flowers, oh arhat!
9. A train is moving rapidly, being pulled by an ardent engine, red as the burning fire of outer space...
10. You must understand the symbol, my child!
11. You must pull a very heavy train with the burning fire of your flaming mind...
12. My child, you must drag this train of human evolution on the spiral tracks of life, until you carry it to the kingdom of the Father.
13. Masicula and Pasiculo, this is how you transform the human being.
14. The fire transforms all. However, the human being cannot possess life if he is not a participant of Gnosis.
15. When the sacred fire departs through Brahmarandra, then the mind of the arhat shines within the burning flames of Mahat.
16. The Auric Egg glows with the terrific fire of the arhat.

17. The aroma of all our innumerable personalities that we have had through the wheel of births and deaths are conserved in this Auric Egg.
18. All of these personalities have died, however their aroma has remained, injected in the Tree of Life (the Innermost) and in the Auric Egg.
19. It is not the human personalities which reincarnate, but the Innermost, the divine triad, the Tree of Life, whose aroma is injected by its passing leaves (passing personalities).
20. The Auric Egg is the protective armor that protects all of our internal vehicles. It is the aura of the Innermost.
21. The Auric Egg is elaborated with the same substance as the Innermost and it now shines with the fire of the arhat.
22. All the wisdom and all the omniscience of the seven Cosmocreators are synthesized with the seven degrees of the power of the fire.
23. You must now completely unite your pineal gland with your pituitary gland by means of the fire.
24. Our karmic debts are registered in the Auric Egg.
25. The Innermost is a true Immolated Lamb who must pay the karma of each one of his passing personalities.
26. Tantric personalities are totally separated from their Innermost and they sink themselves into the Avitchi without being able to inject their aroma into the Tree of Life, into the divine reincarnated triad.
27. In such cases, the eternal triad must revest itself with a new personality in order to continue its cosmic evolution, while its tantric ex-personality is slowly being disintegrated in the Avitchi.
28. In these times, human evolution is a failure. The majority of human personalities are already separated from their Innermost.
29. Only the Innermosts that have not lost their personalities will reincarnate in the Age of Aquarius.
30. The others, the failures, must wait in the internal worlds until the luminous Age of Aquarius passes. The last

opportunity will be given to these personalities in the Age of Capricorn.

31. The dawn of Sagittarius will be definitive. The Innermosts that have then attained dominion over their rebel personalities will assimilate the aroma of their personalities, that is, their psychic extracts, in order to continue their cosmic evolution on the wheel of births and deaths.

32. The failures will totally lose their tantric personalities. After they revest themselves with a new personality they will continue their cosmic evolution as 'remnants'.

33. The tantric ex-personalities of the remnants, who are separated from their superior Being, will slowly disintegrate in the Avitchi.

34. Our reincarnating triad is formed by Atman-Buddhi-Manas. This is the eternal and indestructible triad.

35. This is the Innermost with his two twin souls: the divine soul and the human soul.

36. This is AOM within ourselves.

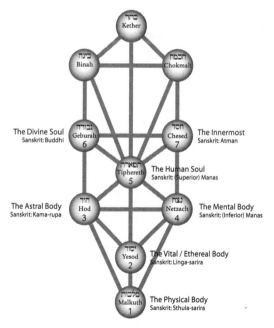

ATMAN-BUDDHI-MANAS ON THE TREE OF LIFE

37. The terrestrial personalities are like the leaves of the marvellous Tree of Life.

38. The sacred fire of the arhat permits us to study all the great mysteries of the fire within the igneous rose of the universe.

39. Everything which we have stated about the Avitchi in this chapter can be synthesized with the following biblical verses:

40. *"He that soweth the good seed is the son of man. The field is the world; the good seed are children of the kingdom; but the tares are the children of the wicked one;*

    "The enemy that sowed them is the devil; the harvest is the end of the world; and the reapers are the angels.

    "As therefore the tares are gathered and burned in the fire; so shall it be in the end of this world.

    "The Son of Man shall send forth his angels, and they shall gather out of his kingdom all things that offend, and them which do iniquity.

    "And shall cast them into a furnace of fire: there shall be wailing and gnashing of teeth.

    "Then shall the righteous shine forth as the sun in the kingdom of their FATHER.. Who hath ears to hear, let him hear." —Matthew 13:37-43

Chapter 25
Diviners and Prophets

1. *"For the idols have spoken vanity, and the diviners have seen a lie, and have told false dreams; they comfort in vain: therefore they went their way as a flock, they were troubled, because there was no shepherd."* –Zechariah 10:2
2. We must make a differentiation between diviners and prophets.
3. Eliphas Levi states the following: "Diviner comes from the words divinaris, divinus, which signifies to perform the 'divine'." Nevertheless, the Abbot Alphonse Louis Constant did not know that the word diviner is "adivino" in Spanish. The letter "a" that precedes the word means "without."
4. Spanish grammar says that the "a" is a preposition that indicates a separation, a disconnection. For example, theos means God, but if we place the letter "a" before it, then we form the word atheos, meaning atheist. The word atheist signifies a person who disbelieves in God. So then, adivino (diviner) precisely represents the contrary of what is divine, in other words, the diabolic. For instance, apolitical signifies "without political attitudes, content or bias."
5. If we carefully read the Bible, we do not find a single word that is in favor of diviners.
6. When the King Nebuchadnezzar commanded that the magicians, the astrologers, the diviners and the enchanters be called in order to interpret his dream with the statue, there was not one single diviner who could interpret this arcanum for the king. Only a prophet from God appeared before the King and said:

"The secret which the king hath demanded cannot the wise men, the astrologers, the magicians, the soothsayers, shew unto the King;

"But there is a God in heaven that revealeth secrets,
and maketh known to the King Nebuchadnezzar
what shall be in the latter days."

7. This is textually taken from the second chapter of the Book of Daniel and it invites us to meditate.

8. Daniel, the prophet of the living God, was the only one who was able to interpret the dream of Nebuchadnezzar.

9. The diviners are tenebrous seers. They are black magicians.

10. The prophets are seers of the light. They are white magicians.

11. The diviners see the images of the abyss and experience dreams of the abyss with which they predict events that do not always crystallize in the physical world.

12. The tenebrous scenes of the abyss are truly in the abyss, but they do not always crystallize in the physical world.

13. The prophets are seers of the light. They are people of God, illuminated by the Holy Spirit. Their predictions are exact because their pineal and pituitary glands are totally illuminated by the sacred fire.

14. The chelas of the White Fraternity are apprentices, disciples of the prophets. This is why they can serve as messengers of the prophets, speaking the words of the holy masters to the human beings.

15. The Holy Spirit is needed in order to be a prophet.

16. However, the disciples of our White Lodge are messengers of the prophets and disciples of the prophets.

17. Vain dreams are from the abyss...

18. Dreams of the light are from the light...

19. There are hierarchies among the prophets...

20. Illumination is achieved little by little because "Nature does not make jumps." There are always scales and scales, degrees and degrees in everything.

21. There exists the seer of the seer and the prophet of the prophet.

22. The seer of the seer is the Innermost. The prophet of the prophet is the Innermost.

23. The luminous visions of our disciples come from the White Hierarchies.
24. However, if our disciples surrender themselves to fornication and take the black path, they walk far from the path of the prophets and they become diviners.
25. Dreams are then dreams from the abyss. They are vain dreams, and their tenebrous predictions lamentably fail.
26. The prophets are masters of the venerable White Lodge.
27. Diviners are the black magicians, tenebrous seers, prophets of the Baalim who eat at Jezebel's table, teaching fornication and how to eat things sacrificed unto idols.
28. Our disciples must follow the path of perfection. They must be pure, pure, pure, so that the very pure crystal of their imagination will be a perfect mirror in which all the precious images of the Universal Fire will be reflected.
29. All impure thoughts, all hatred, all envy, jealousy, evil, etc., overshadow the very pure crystal of clairvoyance, converting our disciples into seers of the shadows, into diviners.

THE EXPULSION FROM EDEN

Chapter 26
The Tree of the Science of Good and Evil

1. *"And the Lord Jehovah said, Behold, the man is become as one of us, to know good and evil: and now, lest he put forth his hand, and take also of the tree of life, and eat, and live for ever:*

   "Therefore the Lord Jehovah sent him forth from the garden of Eden, to till the ground from whence he was taken.

   "So he drove out the man; and he placed at the east of the garden of Eden the cherubim, and a flaming sword which turned every way, to keep the way of the tree of life." —Genesis 3:22-24

2. My child, you have eaten from the tree of the science of good and evil. Therefore, you have known that its fruits are "sweet in the mouth, and bitter in the belly."

3. Now, sibling of mine, you have known the happiness of having a child and the pain of losing it. You enjoyed all the pleasures of the human race. You wallowed as a pig in the mud of the earth, and you drank from all the tempting cups.

4. Now, my child, break the cup of fornication so that you may return to Eden, knowing good and evil as one of us.

5. You have eaten the forbidden fruit for eighteen million years. Now, sibling of mine, you know the taste of that fruit. This is how with great bitterness you have acquired knowledge of good and evil.

6. Now, you must choose not to eat from this forbidden tree, so that you may enter into Eden from where you departed...

7. Once in Eden, you will eat from the other tree of paradise named the "Tree of Life." Thus, you will live forever, and rivers of pure water will flow from your belly...

8. You have suffered greatly, my child. You are an inhabitant of the valley of bitterness. With the sweat of your

face, you have eaten the bread of the earth, and thorns
and thistles have pierced your flesh.

9. So my child, do not eat of that painful fruit! You must
now enter into Eden, through the door from which you
departed...

10. Sibling of mine, do not attempt to break or jump over
the walls of Eden, because you can enter Paradise only
through the doors from which you departed.

11. The human being departed from Paradise through the
door of sex, and only through this door can he enter
Paradise again.

12. Eden is sex itself. Therefore, we can enter Eden only from
where we departed.

13. Vain people will uselessly try to assault the walls of
Eden...

14. We can enter Paradise only through the door through
which we departed... This door is sex.

15. The theorizing spiritual devotees, fornicators, and other
prophets of Baalim who eat at Jezebel's table will uselessly try to break the walls of Eden.

16. My child, you have known Greeks and Romans. You took
part in the biblical Exodus, and the austere priests of all
religions of the earth scarcely offered you a day of consolation...

17. You covered yourself with sackcloth and proclaimed fasts
and penance. The gateways of the temples of all religions
of the earth hardly gave you consolation for your painful
heart. However, the sting of time awoke you from the
hard roughness of existence, even though you did not
find any traveller who could console you along your way.
Catholic or Protestant, Buddhist or Muslim, etc., are now
just withered leaves within your painful heart...

18. You were man, you were woman, and as a woman you
had suitors at the foot of your window... Thus, you
enjoyed orgies and banquets... feasts and uproars...

19. You were a wanderer and a humble beggar woman... an
impoverished elderly woman, and the merchants kicked
you out of their stores with their feet.

20. You were a great matron among perfumes, gold and silk, and each time that death visited you, you then saw the vanity of passing things.

21. Sibling of mine, remember your first love!... Remember from where you departed... and enter through the door of Eden.

22. The door of Eden is sex... and you departed through this door when the Lord Jehovah cast you out for having disobeyed his commandment.

23. Now, my child, you must obey and enter.

    "Open thy doors, O Lebanon, that the fire may devour thy cedars." —Zechariah 11:1

24. *"Thus saith the Lord Jehovah of the Hosts; If thou wilt walk in my ways, and if thou wilt keep my charge, then thou shalt also judge my house, and shalt also keep my courts, and I will give thee places to walk among these that stand by."* —Zechariah 3:7

SYMBOLIC HINDU ILLUSTRATION OF THE FRONTAL CHAKRA (AJNA), WHICH IS RELATED TO CLAIRVOYANCE.

Chapter 27

Clairvoyance

1. In previous chapters we explained divine clairvoyance.
2. Among clairvoyants, there are degrees upon degrees and scales upon scales. This is because illumination is achieved by degrees, little by little.
3. It is necessary to differentiate between the clairvoyance of disciples and the clairvoyance of masters.
4. When the master has risen his first serpent up to the middlebrow, then his Buddhic body receives Buddhic clairvoyance. A star of five points, which radiates an immaculate, white shining light, glows upon the middle-brow of his Buddhic body.
5. When the master has carried his second serpent to the middlebrow, then the frontal chakra of his ethereal body is opened and the master acquires ethereal sight.
6. When the master has made his third serpent reach the frontal chakra of his astral body, he then becomes clair-voyant in the astral world.
7. When the master has made his fourth serpent reach the frontal chakra of the mental body, he then becomes clair-voyant in the mental world. The same happens with the seven degrees of the power of the fire.
8. However, disciples can make their chakras spin. Thus, they will become clairvoyant.
9. This is how disciples prepare themselves for the advent of the fire.
10. A disciple could develop a very potent clairvoyance, yet, if this clairvoyance is compared with the frontal chakra of a master of Major Mysteries, it will be like comparing an insignificant light bulb with the splendorous light of the sun.
11. Oh arhat, the sacred fire of your mental body has opened its way to the frontal chakra of your mind!

12. You have defeated darkness, you have defeated the tenebrous ones, and the door of your frontal chakra is opened...

13. Now, within burning flames of blazing fire, the white dove of the Holy Spirit leaves through that opened door.

14. Receive now a tiny maroon stone... Receive it, sibling... You are now a clairvoyant of Mahat...

15. Enter the temple, sibling of mine, in order to celebrate the feast...

16. Now, my child, it is necessary to unite the mind and the heart by means of fire.

17. The heart and the head must march in perfect equilibrium. The heart and the head must march equilibrated. The heart and the head must march in perfect harmony. This is possible only by uniting the heart and the head by means of fire.

18. From the middlebrow to the heart this is an avenue, a road, and certain secret chambers. Here is where the fire must pass through...

19. Without the power of the fire it is impossible for the heart and the mind to be equilibrated and in harmony.

20. Spiritual devotees from all schools talk about the equilibrium between mind and heart. Yet, without the power of the fire it is impossible for the mind and the heart to be equilibrated.

21. The head and the heart are united only by means of the Kundalini.

22. The fire connects the mind with the divine triad, which resides in the heart.

23. The mind gives us the bread of wisdom when it is connected with the heart by means of the fire.

24. The mental man resides in the head and the heavenly man resides in the heart.

25. It is necessary to unite the mental man with the heavenly man by means of the fire.

26. The Kundalini unites mind and heart.

27. Intellectuals are morally depraved beings because they move themselves only under the direction of the

Guardian of the Threshold of their mental body. They do not hear the voice of the heavenly man who resides in the heart.

28. The mind must convert itself into an instrument of the heart.

29. We must learn how to think with the heart.

30. The mind must flow delectably with the exquisite feeling of the heart.

31. The mind must become lovely and simple.

32. The wisdom of the heart illuminates the mind.

33. The wisdom of the heart is placed in the chalice of the mind as the blood of redemption.

34. The mind of the arhat is symbolized by the Holy Grail.

35. The heart's love is the perfection of wisdom.

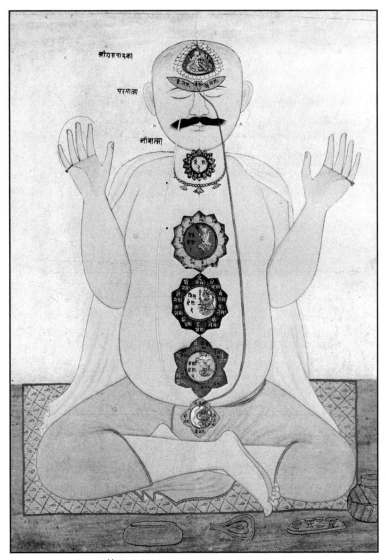

HINDU DRAWING OF THE CHAKRAS AND VITAL CURRENTS

Chapter 28
The Magnetic Field of the Root of the Nose

1. The first chamber of the igneous road that leads from the middlebrow to the heart is in the root of the nose.
2. Knock strongly on the doors of this chamber, oh arhat!
3. Subtle temptations assault you in the world of the cosmic mind [Netzach].
4. Wealth is offered to you, along with erotic opportunities, for your sublime goals.
5. However, you must remain alert like the watchman in the time of war, because these fine ordeals are dangerous, oh arhat!
6. There is a magnetic field in the root of the nose where the solar and lunar atoms of our seminal system come into contact.
7. This contact is possible only by means of sexual magic, because the nasal cavities are intimately related with the church of the coccyx, by means of the two ganglionic cords of our spinal medulla.
8. The yogis of India achieve this contact of solar and lunar atoms in the root of their nose and in their Muladhara chakra by means of pranayama and chastity.
9. When we practice sexual magic intensely, the pure Akasha circulates through the Sushumna channel, and its two solar and lunar currents make contact in the magnetic field of the nose.
10. These are the three vital airs of the Brahmanic cord.
11. These three vital airs are governed by the Innermost, by means of the strength of his willpower.
12. These solar and lunar channels must be totally pure so that the solar and lunar currents can circulate freely through its ganglionic cords, and in order for the pure Akasha of the Sushumna channel to flow freely through the spinal column.

13. This is the reason why every type of fornication is forbidden for Gnostics, as well as for yogis and mystics.

14. When these three vital airs are strengthened by the might of willpower, then fornicators are converted into black magicians. However, the holy and chaste human beings are converted into white magicians.

15. Therefore, Parsival and Omar Cherenzi Lind's course of sexual magic that teaches how to mix these three vital airs with fornication and with "scientific" seminal ejaculation (orgasm) converts human beings into black magicians.

16. During the sexual act, our seminal substance descends into its corresponding cavity... When this seminal substance is spilled, we then lose millions of Christic solar atoms. Instantaneously, these solar atoms are substituted by millions of demonic atoms, which enter into the Brahmanic cord by means of the contractions of the genital orgasmic movements. Thus, if we strengthen the three vital airs of pure Akasha by means of our willpower, then the mixing of Akasha with these demonic atoms, which were collected from the infernos of the human being, result in the awakening of the luciferic serpent (Kundabuffer). Hence, this is a negative and demonic way...

17. Accordingly, with the awakening of tantric powers, the inferior quaternary ends by divorcing itself from the divine triad. This is how that quaternary converts itself into a perverse demon of the abyss.

18. This separation is done when the bridge known as Antahkarana is broken. This cord connects the inferior quaternary with the divine triad.

19. The Antahkarana corresponds to the umbilical cord of the fetus.

20. The tenebrous and negative sexual magic of the black magician Omar Cherenzi Lind and the traitor Parsival Krumm-Heller mixes the satanic atoms, which are collected by the sexual organs after the tantric ejaculation (orgasm), with the three vital airs and fortifies them.

This is how they awake the igneous serpent in the negative way (the Kundabuffer).

21. This is how the disciples of Cherenzi Lind and the disciples of the traitor Parsival are separated from their divine triad, and how they convert themselves into perverse demons.

22. A movement of Akashic circulation is established from Shushumna, Ida, and Pingala that flows through the entire body.

23. The magnetic field of the nose is a battlefield and a place of vigilance.

24. The defensive atoms of the organism have their place of vigilance in this field, that impedes the entering of indolent and malignant atoms, which produce many types of sicknesses.

25. The Transformation atoms and the Aspiring atoms of our organism enter through this magnetic field in order to place themselves under the service of the Nous atom of the heart.[14]

26. All the processes of the great initiations are performed in the secret, ardent chambers of the Shushumna channel.

27. The four great initiations of Major Mysteries are: Srotapanna, Sakridagamin, Anagamin, Arhan[15]. These are the four paths that lead to Nirvana.

28. However, even when the arhat is an adept, he must still raise the fifth, sixth and seventh serpents of his eternal divine triad, in order to convert himself into an arhat of the "mist of fire."

29. These are the seven great initiations of Major Mysteries.

30. There are the seven serpents that the human being must raise by intensely practicing sexual magic with his spouse. They can also be raised by means of the strength of the sacrifice of a total and definitive sexual abstention, as performed by the authentic yogis who follow the path

---

14   These terms are from *The Dayspring of Youth* by M.

15   These are Sanskrit versions of the Pali words Sotapanna, Sakadagami, Anagami, and Arahat, and are four paths described by Buddha Shakyamuni.

of perfection, or as performed by the sublime mystics, Ramakrishna, Francis of Assisi, or Anthony of Padua.

31. The masters of the seventh ardent scale are only one step from the fundamental root of their hierarchy.

32. This fundamental root of the White Hierarchy is found enclosed in the "Baniano Humano."

33. This marvelous being is the master of masters of the great White Lodge. He is Sanat Kumara, the founder of the College of Initiates of the universal White Fraternity.

34. He is one of the Four Thrones, of which the Bible speaks.

35. This great being descended to our Earth in the beginning of the Lemurian epoch, before the separation of sexes, in order to found the College of Initiates of the great hierarchy. He has been incarnated in a physical body since that time, without death having any power over him. He lives in Asia.

36. The arhat who arrives to the world of the "mist of fire" is one step towards the eighth and ninth initiations of the fundamental root of the hierarchy.

37. These heights are reached by practicing sexual magic, or by vowing to a total and definitive abstention, and by walking the path of perfect holiness.

38. Karma is not an obstacle for this, because we can pay all our debts by sacrificing even the last drop of our blood in favor of all the human beings who populate the entire face of the Earth.

39. *"Behold, happy is the man whom God correcteth: therefore despise not thou the chastening of the Almighty."* –Job 5:17

40. Whosoever has capital to pay, pays and does well in his negotiations.

41. Perform good deeds so that you may pay your debts.

42. When an inferior law is transcended by a superior law, the superior law washes away the inferior law.

43. The lion of the law is fought with the scale.

44. Therefore, the human being can break his chains in the hour that he wishes. He can rise the seven ardent scales, and can convert himself into a dragon of wisdom within the "mist of fire."

45. The primordial atom, **Anu**, is the purest atom that enters through the magnetic field of our nose. This atom cannot be multiplied in the pre-genetic or primal-genetic state. It is an omni-gatherer. It is omniscient, omnipresent, a total sum, unlimited and absolutely divine.

46. All the atomic activity of the magnetic field of the nose and the chakra Muladhara is based on this atom.

47. The Fohat selects all the atoms which must penetrate through our nasal cavities.

48. The Fohat combines the distinct atomic elements for our divine goals.

49. Each human being possesses its own Fohat, and the total addition of all the Fohats constitute the universal Fohat, the universal fire of life, whose intelligent flames combine the atomic elements of space in order to fecundate the chaotic matter.

50. *"The Mother sleeps, yet is ever breathing."* —The Secret Doctrine

51. Each atom of the cosmos is condemned to incessant differentiations. Only **Anu** does not admit differentiations.

52. *"The Breath of the Father-Mother issues cold and radiant and gets hot and corrupt, to cool once more, and be purified in the eternal bosom of inner Space."* —The Secret Doctrine

53. Everything breathes; everything flows and ebbs; everything inhales and exhales.

54. Every phenomenon of respiration is based on the respiration of the Absolute.

55. The Absolute inhales and exhales.

56. Each exhalation of the Absolute is a cosmic day, and each inhalation of the Absolute is a cosmic night.

57. When the heart of our solar system began to palpitate after the great cosmic night, it continued to repeat the inhalation and the exhalation of the Absolute within the seven "laya" centers. The chaotic masses of these centers were fecundated by the Fohat in order for the seven worlds of our solar system to emanate from the Chaos.

58. This respiration of the Absolute is repeated in the atom, in the ant, in the eagle, and in the human being.

59. Everything flows and ebbs; everything comes and goes; everything pulses and pulses again with this rhythm of divine respiration.

60. During the first dynasties of the pharaohs of ancient Egypt, I received the code of sexual magic in a sacred room of an ancient pyramid blackened by the sun of the desert.

61. The master dressed with his white tunic was standing near a vertical rod, which symbolically represented the phallus.

62. He carefully instructed me about the great mysteries of sex, with the solemn and austere voice of the hierophants.

63. While seated upon a chair, I attentively listened to the hierophant.

64. Then, directing his penetrating eyes towards me, with a loud and authoritative voice, he told me: "Uncover your che-che-re." I then uncovered my sexual organ, and the master told me, from lips to ear, the once unspeakable secret of the Great Arcanum, which consists of sexually connecting oneself with the spouse and withdrawing from her without seminal ejaculation, which means, to restrain the sexual act.

65. I then practiced my first ritual of sexual magic with my priestess, under the direction of the hierophant.

66. "This is marvellous," I exclaimed.

67. Whosoever violated this unspeakable secret, which is the Great Arcanum, was then condemned to death. His head was cut off. His heart was torn out and his ashes were thrown into the four winds.

68. When the semen is not spilled, then the restrained desire causes our seminal energy to rise, filled with billions of Christic atoms. With their light and splendor these Christic atoms illuminate the three channels where the pure Akasha circulates.

69. The mixture of these Christic atoms (which are the result of our semen transmuted into energy), when combined with the pure Akasha, awakens the Kundalini positive-

ly, and opens its way upwards towards Brahmarandra, through the thirty-three chambers of our spinal column. This is how adepthood is achieved.

70. I educated myself at the feet of the great hierophants and i knew the ancient wisdom of the ancient sages of the temple of the mysteries.

71. This is why I feel nothing but infinite pity when presently I see these tiny human beings of this twentieth century "mystically" fornicating.

72. The Akashic breath penetrates through our nasal cavities and descends through our Brahmanic cord.

73. When the Akasha is reinforced by our willpower and by the willpower of the cosmic hierarchies, then it descends from above, from the heavens of Urania and it is precipitated within the profundity of our reed, producing the hissing sound of the sssssssss.

74. Thus, when this Akashic breath collides with the solar and lunar currents and with the Christic atoms that form the Kundalini, the sacred fire then rises one more vertebra, one more canyon in its ascension through the thirty-three canyons until reaching Brahmarandra.

75. When the Akashic breath, reinforced by willpower, descends through our Brahmanic cord and finds atoms of fornication (satanic atoms collected from the infernos of the human being during the movements of the genital orgasmic contraction, which occurs in the seminal ejaculation) instead of Christic atoms, the collision of the Akasha with such satanic atoms awakens the Kundalini in a negative way (awakening the Kundabuffer). A satanic atom that resides in the Muladhara chakra enters into activity, and controls it, causing it to descend from the coccyx downwards towards the atomic infernos of the human being, forming the famous tail with which Satan is represented (the Kundabuffer).

76. The sexual organs collect satanic atoms of the secret enemy with the genital orgasmic contraction during the seminal ejaculation (tantric orgasm), which is advised by the black magician Omar Cherenzi Lind and by the

lost and tenebrous Parsival Krumm-Heller. Therefore, when these atoms attempt to ascend upwardly towards Urania, they then are violently rejected by the Akashic breath, which throws them downwards towards the coccyx. This sexual practice awakens the Muladhara negatively and causes a certain atom of the secret enemy to enter into activity. This atom then exercises control over the Kundalini, directing it downwards towards the submerged worlds of consciousness, thus forming the famous (Kundabuffer) tail of demons.

77. This is how the disciples of these black magicians separate themselves from the divine triad, Atman-Buddhi-Manas. This is how they convert themselves into tantric personalities of the abyss.

78. The Akasha is not the ether, as many believe.

79. The Akasha is the cause of sound, the spiritual cause of the word, the Anima-Mundi, the divine, the divine hierarchies, whose breath enters through the magnetic field of our nose.

80. This is why the sacred scriptures say that God blew a breath of life into the nose of Adam and He infused a living soul into him.

81. *"And the Lord Jehovah formed man of the dust of the ground, and breathed into his nostrils the breath of life; and the man became a living soul."* —Genesis 2:7

Chapter 29

The First Holy Chamber of the Root of the Nose

1. You have defeated subtle ordeals, oh arhat!
2. Now, sibling of mine, enter into the first holy chamber that leads from the middlebrow to the heart.
3. You have begun to unite the mind with the heart.
4. Now, sibling of mine, enter into the temple in order to celebrate the feast.
5. Be joyful, oh heart, sing, child of mine...
6. Finally, after many centuries... the mind and the heart will be united.
7. Sing, oh heart, because your mind has been humbled before the majesty of the Innermost.
8. Sing, oh heart, because the mind advances within the burning fire towards you.
9. Sing, oh heart, because wisdom will now convert into love.
10. You have entered the holy chamber of the magnetic field of the root of your nose...
11. The temple is in festivity, my child, because the ship of your mind is coming from the other shore to the ineffable beaches of Eden, where the rivers of the pure water of life flow with milk and honey.
12. Sing, oh heart, sing, because the rebel house of Israel has been afflicted and humbled before its God.
13. Sing, oh heart... sing, because your sailing ship advances towards the port of light...
14. Sing, oh heart, because your mind is now liberated from all types of schools, religions, orders, sects, lodges, classrooms, concepts of mother countries and flags, prejudice, desires, fears, hatred, envy, intellectualism, sophism, theories, etc.

15. Intellectualism can only conduce humans towards black magic because it is always accompanied with pride and selfishness.

16. Are not perhaps the proud ones, are not perhaps the erudite ones of spiritualism indeed those who have always criticized and attacked us and who have angrily torn up our books?

17. Intellect by itself only conduces humans towards black magic.

18. Those who always criticize, refute, and attack us do so only because they are moved by their pride, selfishness and vanity.

19. Master H.P. Blavatsky knew adepts of average intelligence, but they were adepts.

20. The powers of the masters emanate from their purity of life and the merits of their heart.

21. The powers of the master emanate from his internal God and from harmony with nature and the law.

22. When the personal ego restores itself in its divine eternal triad after each reincarnation and abandons the mental body, it is disintegrated and its atoms remain scattered in the mental plane.

23. These mental atoms are attracted again when the Innermost reconstructs a new mental body in order to enter through the doors of a new reincarnation in the school of life.

24. These manasic atoms, "Tanha causes," and other types, are of the same nature of manas, meaning, they are of the same nature of the mental body. They begin to arrange the atomic structures of this new mental body.

25. Our karma is enclosed within these atoms.

26. This process is repeated through millions of births and deaths.

27. When these atoms of the mind are united with the Innermost by means of the fire of the fourth serpent, we then liberate ourselves from the wheel of births and deaths.

28. Nevertheless, in order to be a Nirvani without residue, we must liberate ourselves from the good karma and from the bad karma.
29. We must not owe, nor should others owe us.
30. As long as the lions of the law owe us something, we are "Nirvanis with residue."
31. As long as we owe something, we are Nirvanis with residue.
32. We must pass beyond good and evil. We must pass beyond intelligence, and even beyond the ineffable spheres of love.
33. We can rise to the summits of light only on the steps of love and sacrifice.
34. We must perform a lot of good deeds for love of humanity.
35. This is how we pay our debts.
36. Later, the lords of the law must also pay the balance in our favor...
37. In the end, we liberate ourselves from the good karma and the bad karma, and we convert ourselves into Nirvanis without residue.
38. The mind must be united with its divine triad, together with the psychic extractions of the astral, vital, and physical vehicles.
39. This is how our triad is reinforced by its inferior quaternary.
40. The inferior **manas** together with the kamas, prana, and linga[16] reinforce the divine triad by means of fire.
41. For these transcendental goals, we utilize from the same mind only its psychic extract.
42. When he is capable of conversing with his Innermost front to front, face to face, the human being reaches the state of Turiya.
43. Many ask themselves, "How is the Innermost? What figure does he have?" etc.

---

16   These Sanskrit terms are references to the four inferior bodies: manas (mind: Netzach), kama (desire: emotion, astral body, Hod), prana (energy: Yesod), linga (spot, mark, sign, gender, idol: Malkuth).

44. The more humble and simple a person is, the more easily he can comprehend the nature of his divine, eternal triad.
45. However, intellectuals can only comprehend the divine triad with the geometrical figure of the triangle.
46. When the mind is united with the heart, then the mind lives within the triad and it is totally nourished by the triad.
47. Nevertheless, the union of the mind with the heart is possible only by means of the fire.

Chapter 30
The Ardent Way

1. The igneous way that leads from the middlebrow to the heart is governed by an atomic god of infinite power.
2. Advance with firm steps towards the second chamber of this ardent way, oh arhat!
3. Fine temptations pursue you...
4. Liquors and pleasures are offered to you, which appear unavoidable.
5. The great monster of jealousy subtly assaults you in the world of flames.
6. Advance, arhat! Remain alert and vigilant like the watchman in the time of war.
7. This ardent way that leads from the middlebrow to the heart is very narrow and very difficult and it is filled with very subtle temptations.
8. The most dangerous matter is the painful past of your life that is mixed with subtle temptations.
9. You must remain firm against those subtle dangers...
10. The more fine a temptation, the more dangerous it is.
11. During these ordeals, you must demonstrate complete equilibrium of the mind and heart.
12. You approach the second chamber of the igneous way that leads from the middlebrow to the heart.
13. My child, you have triumphed over the ordeals.
14. A group of angels joyfully celebrate your victory...
15. You have gained the right to enter Nirvana.
16. You have gained the right to enter the cavalry of the army of Heaven.
17. Enter your chamber, my child, in order to celebrate your feast. You are a Nirvani.
18. You have entered the ineffable joy of Nirvana and all the divine hierarchies are filled with happiness because of your triumph.
19. You are now a blessed one.

SYMBOLIC HINDU ILLUSTRATION OF THE THROAT CHAKRA (VISHUDDHA).

Chapter 31
The Creative Larynx

1. You have reached the splendorous flower of your creative larynx.
2. The word of the gods expresses itself through the creative larynx.
3. Hadit has flourished in your fertile lips made word.
4. Hadit is the winged serpent of Kundalini.
5. The esoteric name of Kundalini is **Solu-sigi-sig**.
6. This is also the name of the central sun.
7. Each one of these letters should be vocalized in the following order.
8. *Sssss Ooooo Luuuu — Sssss Iiiiii Ggggg Iiiiii — Sssss Iiiiii Ggggg*
9. Every letter must be vocalized, prolonging the sound of each letter, just as we have indicated.
10. It is important to prolong the sound of each vowel.
   The vowel "S" is like a sweet and affable hiss. The Bible speaks to us of this sweet and affable hiss in the following verses:

   "And he said, Go forth, and stand upon the mount before Jehovah. And, behold, Jehovah passed by, and a great and strong wind rent the mountains, and brake in pieces the rocks before Jehovah; but Jehovah was not in the wind; and after the wind an earthquake; but Jehovah was not in the earthquake:

   "And after a earthquake a fire: but Jehovah was not in the fire: and after the fire a still small voice (hiss).

   "And it was so, when Elijah heard it, that he wrapped his face in his mantle, and went out, and stood in the entering in of the cave. And, behold, there came a voice (hiss) unto him, and said, what doest thou here, Elijah?" —1 Kings:19:11-13

11. The "S," as a mantra, permits us to leave our cave (physical body) and to enter upon the mount (astral plane).

12. The vowel "S" is a mantra for projection of the astral body.
13. The disciple must become sleepy while vocalizing the sweet and affable sound of the "S." When the disciple reaches that state of transition between vigil and dream, then he must rise from his bed and leave the room, going towards the Gnostic Church.
14. Once in the Gnostic Church, we will teach and instruct him in the divine wisdom.
15. However, we must clarify to our disciples that this explanation which we have given must be understood as an immediate action.
16. The student must rise up from his bed, as naturally as would a child who knows nothing of esotericism. It is not a mental practice. It is a practice which must be understood as a concrete action, just as when we rise up in the morning in order to eat breakfast.
17. The vowel "S" has a terrific power.
18. The vowel "S" is the rune Sig and when we vocalize it, lightning is produced in the internal atmosphere. This lightning has the power to awaken the Kundalini.
19. The sexual organ of the future divine humanity will be the creative larynx.
20. The throat is a uterus in which the word is created.
21. The Kundalini gives the larynx the entire omnipotent power of the creative word.
22. What is important is to learn how to control the feminine principle of the solar forces.
23. The feminine solar forces are symbolized by an eagle with a woman's head.
24. Sexual magic is the way.
25. We must Self-realize Christ within ourselves in order to speak the creative word. However, this is possible only by learning how to control the feminine principle of the sun.
26. We know that sexual magic is very hard and difficult for humans with a weak will. Therefore, we recommend our disciples to first practice the exercises of the rune Thorn,

in order to acquire the force of willpower, which will permit them to heroically control sexual magic.

27. Our disciples must perform this exercise by placing their hand upon their waist or hip and then vocalizing the syllables **Ti-Te-To-Tu-Ta**, prolonging the sound of each vowel. They must then vocalize the mantra Thorn as follows: **Tooooooorrrrrrrrrnnnnnnnnn.**

28. Our disciples who practice this exercise daily will acquire a powerful force of will, with which they will practice sexual magic, dominating their passionate beast.

RUNE THORN

29. Willpower's strength is symbolized by the crown of thorns of the Nazarene Christ.

30. It is necessary to strike the hard flint strongly in order to make the spark of immortality jump.

31. Willpower's strength is the tremendous force of sacrifice... It is the crown of thorns of the master.

32. The will and movement of the Kundalini are intimately united.

33. Willpower's strength is the rune Thorn and its movement is symbolized by the sign Olin of the Aztec Mexicans.

34. The runes Thorn and Olin enclose the secret of our liberation.

RUNE OLIN

35. It is necessary to have the strength of willpower in order to place the Kundalini into motion.

36. The hierarchies related with the elemental department of the cedar tree have the power to open the door of Olin.

37. This door is situated in the inferior orifice of the spinal medulla, and through it we enter the great mysteries of the fire.

38. The mantra that opens this door is Thorn. It is pronounced by prolonging the sound of each vowel as follows: Toooorrrrnnnnnn.

JESUS WITH HIS CROWN OF THORNS AND HIS STAFF OF MASTERY

"Willpower's strength is the tremendous
force of sacrifice... It is the crown
of thorns of the master."

39. The mantra Thorn has the power to place the pure Akasha into motion in order to awaken the Kundalini and to make it rise through each one of the thirty-three vertebrae of our spinal column.

40. This mantra has the power to reinforce the pure Akasha within our Brahmanic cord.

41. Olin, the sacred sign of the Aztec Indians, is the door to enter into the great mysteries of the fire.

42. The exercise of Olin must be performed by placing the right arm upon the waist [figure a]. Then, while vocalizing the mantra Thorn, both arms must be extended towards the left side of the body [figure b] and at the end, both arms must be placed upon the waist [figure c].

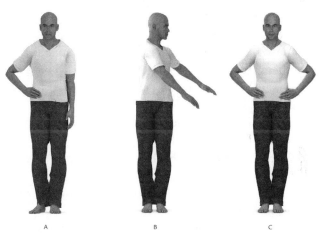

A   B   C

THE EXERCISE OF RUNE OLIN

43. The vocalization must be combined with inhalations and exhalations of pure air with the intention of carrying the vital Christ to each of the seven bodies.

44. The sign Olin is governed by the sign of Scorpio, which controls the sexual organs.

45. We know that the whole power of the Kundalini is found in the phallus and in the uterus. The secret for awakening the Kundalini is contained in the union of the two.

46. On one occasion, when conversing with a master of the
    great White Hierarchy, he touched my sexual organs
    in order to examine me. I then felt an electric shock
    throughout my body. The master was very content and
    said to me, "You are progressing very well."
47. Nature has its origin in the fire and the entire power of
    the fire is found enclosed within our sexual organs.
48. In his course of *Magic Runes*, Master Huiracocha teaches
    all these things. However, sacred runes are not the prop-
    erty of Master Huiracocha, because this knowledge is as
    ancient as the world. It belongs to the great schools of
    internal mysteries.
49. We do not accept the statement of Master Huiracocha
    that black and yellow skinned people cannot belong to
    the White Lodge because it is only for people who belong
    to the white race.
50. We cannot accept this type of racial prejudice, because
    the White Lodge is universal.
51. There are masters from all races in our venerable White
    Lodge. We must not forget that Master Moria and
    Master Kout Humi belong to the yellow race.
52. The white race is not superior nor inferior than other
    races. Simply, it is different, that is all.
53. We also disagree with Master Huiracocha's despise for
    Asian wisdom.
54. Christ taught three ways to reach the union with the
    Innermost.
55. When he was preaching to the multitudes, when he was
    mystically exalted, he showed us the way of Ramakrishna,
    Kempis, and Francis of Assisi. This is the path of
    Anthony of Padua and Theresa of Jesus. This is the mys-
    tical path.
56. When Christ was walking with Magdalene, the repented
    prostitute, when he was among publicans and sinners,
    fishermen and wine drinkers, he showed us the Gnostic
    path.

57. When he retired to the solitude of the desert for forty days and forty nights, he then taught the way of Asian yoga.
58. The seven rays of cosmic evolution are synthesized in these three ways that the Nazarene showed.
59. Therefore, we cannot despise Asian wisdom.
60. All human Innermosts who are fastened to the wheel of births and deaths belong to these three ways.
61. With all this, we sustain that sexual magic between husband and wife is the way in order to reach Nirvana.
62. Therefore, we cannot accept the racial prejudice of Master Huiracocha for any reason.
63. God has no preference for anyone. All human beings without distinction of sex, race, creed, or color are beloved children of the Father. They have the same rights.
64. We also cannot accept the absurd thesis of Master Huiracocha who stated that it is a sin for a man of one race to become married with a woman of another race, and that the bastard children are children of the devil.
65. We recognize that Master Huiracocha is a guru of the universal White Fraternity. It is evident for me that he is an archbishop of the Gnostic Church. Yet, he committed a lamentable mistake when he made these statements in his course of *Magic Runes*.
66. There is no doubt that if the Guru Huiracocha had a physical body he would rectify those errors. Humans commit errors, however only those who are stubborn remain in the error.
67. *"Be thou, oh Hadit, the Gnostic secret of my Being, the central point of my connection and flourish in my fertile lips made word."*
68. When the Kundalini of the mental body reaches the rose of the creative larynx, a trumpet of the temple resounds in the internal worlds. Then, we enter the temple in order to celebrate the feast.
69. All human beings — white, black, yellow, red and brown — have the right to speak the word of light and to form

part of the great, universal White Fraternity, because everyone is a beloved child of the Father.

70. God has no preference for anyone. He equally cares for humans and ants, birds and reptiles.

71. God has no racial prejudice. He loves all his children with infinite love, without distinction of sex, race, creed, or color.

72. We must love all human beings. We must give even the last drop of our blood for all our brothers and sisters who belong to this great human family.

73. Evil ones criticize me because I teach the secret doctrine of Gnostics to humanity.

74. I diffuse all the esoteric teachings in order to save all my brothers and sisters of this humanity.

75. Everything that I know is for my brothers and sisters. Therefore, I have decided to teach them the most sacred things of the universe, so that they may enter Eden, as I have entered.

Chapter 32

The Fourth Chamber

1. You have reached the fourth chamber of the narrow way that leads from the middlebrow to the heart. This chamber is situated beneath the thyroid gland, above the sternum (breastbone), the superior part of the rib cage.
2. Fine temptations have assaulted you in the world of the cosmic mind. You have comprehended how crime is hidden within spirituality.
3. You have understood that crime is also hidden within the incense of prayer.
4. You have also seen how crime is hidden among the pleroma of a spiritual fraternity.
5. You have seen, oh sibling of mine, how refined, mental adultery with a tinge of transcendental spirituality can emerge from a simple spiritual friendship between two beings of opposite sexes.
6. Now, my child, you are comprehending in what form and in what manner the mind and the heart are united and equilibrated by means of the fire.
7. A door has been opened. Enter my child, in order to celebrate your feast.
8. The instant has arrived, sibling of mine, in which you must be more concerned with music.
9. The orchestras of Eden resound in the infinite spaces, within the great rhythms.
10. The entire universe is supported by the magnificent orchestration of the spheres.

ANUBIS BALANCES THE SCALE

"The god Anubis, jackal-headed, tests the tongue of the balance, the suspending bracket of which is in the form of the feather. The inscription above the head of Anubis reads:--"He who is in the tomb saith, pray thee, O weigher of righteousness, to guide (?) the balance that it may be stablished.'" - E. A. Wallis Budge, The Papyrus of Ani

Chapter 33
The Fifth Chamber

1. You have entered the fifth ardent chamber of the narrow way that leads from the middlebrow to the heart.
2. A door has been opened. Enter, my child!
3. Listen now, oh arhat, what the angel is reading from the book.
4. Many sublime things related with the world of the cosmic mind are now being taught to you.
5. You are acting intensely in the world of pure spirit without the necessity of material vehicles.
6. All the principal teachings have been given to you in sacred language.
7. The sun has shone upon the tree of your life and you have entered the fifth chamber.
8. You see, sibling of mine, how you are approaching the sacred temple of the heart.
9. Now you are understanding how to equilibrate the mind and heart.
10. As time passes, you become more aware of how you can act with complete consciousness within your superior Being without the necessity of the four bodies of sin.
11. Truly, child of mine, you are an arhat. You are a Nirvani.
12. You are a master of Major Mysteries. Yet, in the world of Nirvana, you have now begun to live as a disciple of the gods.
13. You are a master and you are a disciple. You have learned how to obey and how to command...
14. You are a super-human.
15. My child, you have built a majestic temple in the astral world and in the mental world, but in the world of Nirvana, you possess only a tiny, little chapel.
16. When will you have a great cathedral within Nirvana?
17. When will you be an inhabitant of the seventh salon of Nirvana?

18. When will you live in that great city of gold of the seventh salon of Nirvana?
19. Behold the ineffable beings who officiate in their great cathedrals of Nirvana.
20. When will you be as one of them?
21. Sibling of mine, now you have only a tiny, little chapel in the first sub-plane of Nirvana.
22. My child, you are now a beginner in Nirvana!
23. Duty is much harder for you now, oh arhat!
24. If you want to progress in Nirvana, then you must sacrifice yourself for humanity.
25. Sibling of mine, you must become a bodhisattva of compassion.
26. Each one of your sacrifices will be paid unto you in Nirvana.
27. Thus, sibling of mine, this is the only way in order for you to progress in Nirvana.
28. You see, sibling of mine, how the fire has transformed you.
29. You see, sibling of my soul, that you, hidden within your sexual organs, carried all the secrets of Nirvana.
30. You suffered indescribably when searching for Nirvana. You were affiliated to various schools, religions, lodges, and orders. Yet, they gave you only one day of consolation.
31. You, child of mine, proclaimed penance and covered your body with sackcloth, but in vain.
32. You, sibling of my soul, forgot the door of Eden. This is why you suffered.
33. But, you saw that Nirvana was in your sexual organs.
34. What a lot of tasks, child of mine!
35. However, you finally saw the door of Eden within your sexual organs. Thus, this is how you entered...

Chapter 34
The Sixth Chamber

1. You are now descending little by little, sibling of mine, through the interior of your temple, from the tower to the heart.
2. You are seated at the window of the base of your tower.
3. You are in the interior of your temple, sibling of mine, and you descend little by little from the cupola to the sacred sanctuary of your heart.
4. The profundity of the floor of the temple is seen from the height of the internal window...
5. The height causes vertigo, sibling of mine...
6. Woe to the arhat who does not know how to control the vertigo of height, because he will fall into the abyss...
7. Whosoever has understanding, let him understand, and whosoever has ears, let him hear what I am saying to the arhats.
8. You are very high, oh arhat! An ineffable chorus rises up to your window, from the profundities of your sanctuary.
9. The masters delectably sing in a sacred language...
10. Persevere, oh arhat, be cautious, be prudent and do not become conceited with the vertigo of heights.
11. Be humble, sibling of mine, be perfect, as your Father who is in heaven is perfect.
12. Enter your sixth chamber, sibling of mine.
13. This chamber is formed by crossing halls.
14. This chamber belongs to the Sixth Arcanum of the Tarot: The Lovers.
15. Do you remember your errors?

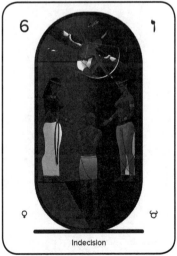

Indecision

ARCANUM SIX

16. Do you remember, sibling of mine, the tenebrous epochs of your life, when you were experiencing in yourself the Sixth Arcanum of the Tarot?

17. Do you remember the times when you were wandering along the crooked ways of adultery and fornication?

18. Enter now, sibling of mine, into this chamber illuminated by the light of your candlestick.

19. Receive your painful memories with patience... Receive your warnings with patience.

20. Receive your feast, oh arhat!

Chapter 35
The Seventh Chamber

1. You are now before the door of the seventh chamber, oh arhat!
2. This chamber is symbolized by the Seventh Arcanum of the Tarot: The Chariot of War.
3. Remember your first love, sibling of mine. Remember your Divine Mother, the blessed goddess mother of the world, who you abandoned when you ate the forbidden fruit.
4. Did she indeed not love you? What were you lacking, sibling of mine? Why did you abandon your mother?
5. Knock, ungrateful child, knock strongly upon the door of the seventh chamber so that it will be opened unto you.
6. Disobedient child, repent of your ungratefulness. Cry, lament, and fight indescribably so that the gods will open the door of this chamber for you.
7. This is the Seventh Arcanum of the Tarot. You must fight a lot, sibling of mine, in order for the gods to open the door of this chamber for you.
8. The Seventh Arcanum of the Tarot is represented by a chariot of war pulled by two sphinxes, one white and the other black.
9. The white sphinx symbolizes the blessed goddess mother of the world, and the black sphinx symbolizes the shadow of the Divine Mother, Hekate, Proserpine, the queen of the atomic infernos of

Triumph

ARCANUM SEVEN

nature, the black goddess who is greatly adored by the demons of darkness.

10. You abandoned your mother by following this tenebrous goddess of carnal passions. Now, you must repent for your ungratefulness and knock strongly upon the door of the seventh chamber in order for the gods to open it for you.

11. Enter with your chariot of war, oh arhat! Knock strongly so that they will open the door for you.

12. The door has been opened. Now, enter your chamber, oh arhat!

13. Enter the seventh chamber and receive your feast.

14. You are a child. Powerful weapons have been given to you. If you do not know how to use them, you will hurt others and yourself.

Chapter 36

The Eighth Chamber

1. Knock strongly on your temple, oh arhat!
2. Be joyful, sibling of mine, be joyful since you have reached the goal of your heart.
3. The specialist who awoke your fourth serpent and who with supreme efforts, wisely conduced your serpent to those sacred centers of your heart, has been paid.
4. Every work must be paid for, and your specialist has been paid for this grandiose service, which is to have wisely conduced your serpent from the coccyx to the ineffable chambers of your heart.
5. Only unselfish service, chastity, and sanctity take us to the ineffable summits.
6. Now, sibling of mine, you have seen what the great service is.
7. I know many spiritual brothers and sisters, good and virtuous, who fight for their perfection.
8. I know many brothers and sisters who fight indescribably to correct their defects and to purify themselves. Yet, they do not remember others... They feel alone, they fight for their own spiritual progress and for their moral self-development. However, they do not remember that they have brothers and sisters, and that all of us are children of the same mother.
9. Their spirituality is selfish spirituality. Therefore, the masters do not owe them anything. There is nothing to pay them because nothing is owed to them. They do not assist anyone. They do not sacrifice themselves for anyone, nor do they fight for the spirituality of anyone.
10. Every initiation is a payment that must be given to the human being. Yet, if nothing is owed to the human being, then nothing is given to him. Therefore, even if he screams and cries out asking for an initiation, he will become old before receiving it.

11. The majestic door of the sacred temple of your heart is opened.
12. Enter, sibling of mine, into the great cathedral of the soul in order to celebrate the feast of the arhat.
13. Enter, sibling of mine, into the heart temple, so you may receive the Fourth Initiation of Major Mysteries.
14. Wear your best clothes... The temple is at feast, because the mind and the heart are united by means of the fire.
15. Some ineffable maidens dance the sacred dance of the runes before you.
16. Your mind hangs from a beam! It is Christified! And it is now unfastened from the cross in order to celebrate the feast.
17. Your mind is now a living Christ. Your mind shines with the sacred power of the fire.
18. Ineffable music resounds in the divine places.
19. The fire of the arhat shines within the sacred chamber of your heart.
20. You now carry Christ within your heart, and the white dove of the Holy Spirit has formed its abode in your heart temple.
21. Ineffable angels carry the long train of your cloak... The beautiful maidens dance the dance of the runes.
22. The king of the world, seated upon his throne, awaits you, sibling of mine!
23. Sanat Kumara, dressed with a ceremonial vesture, delivers the sacred symbol of Mercury to you.
24. You are an imperator of the mind, you are an arhat of thought.
25. Your mind now burns ardently within the sparks of the universal flames.
26. Your mind now shines within the igneous rose of the universe.
27. You have liberated yourself from the illusion of separatism. You are *That... That... That...*
28. You live in all hearts. You see through all eyes. You hear through all ears, because you are *That...That... That...*
29. You can now exclaim: "I am Atman, the ineffable."

30. "I am what I am. I am the one who has always been, the one who will always be.

31. "The entire starry infinite is my body... The entire universe is my personality. This is why I express myself with strength and power, through my arhats...

32. "I cry in the child. I sing in the bird and I flourish in my pomegranates."

33. Now you must understand, sibling of mine, the personality within impersonality.

34. Now you must comprehend, sibling of mine, that the illusion of separation is a heresy, and that the selfish personality of those who only want to be themselves, and nothing more than themselves, is the worst of the heresies.

35. When I, Aun Weor, affirm that we must have a strong and potent "I" and a powerful and robust personality, I am not referring to the selfish personality, nor to the animal "I"... I am referring only to the divine "I" and to our gigantic personality formed by all the beings of the infinite.

36. Atman thunders and flashes in all the infinite spaces and manifests himself with potency through his arhats.

37. Atman the ineffable has no weaknesses. He expresses himself with power and majesty through his prophets.

38. Our "I" is universal, and all the bodies of all the living beings are the bodies of our internal and divine "I."

39. When we have spoken of a strong and powerful personality, many have not understood the personality within impersonality. Thus, they have fallen into the horrible heresy of separation.

40. Brothers and sisters of mine, do not let yourselves be guided by the selfish personality of your mental body, nor by your animal intellect.

41. You must listen only to the Innermost who resides in the heart. You must learn to hear the voice of the silence.

42. When we speak of a universal "I," we do not fall into the absurdity of Annie Besant who forgot the individuality of the Innermost.

43. We recognize the individuality within the unity of life, and although we know that the drop sinks into the ocean, we also know that the ocean sinks into the drop.

44. Atman is one who expresses himself as many. The ardent sea of life, free in its movement, has many flames.

45. However, all the flames, when joined, form the sea of ardent fire... the world of the mist of fire.

46. The Innermost is individual and universal at the same time.

47. "I am the flame that burns in each human heart, as it burns in each grain and in the nucleus of each star.

48. "I am the tree, the stone, the bird, the man, the light, the bread, and the wine."

Chapter 37
The Seven Centers of the Heart

1. There are seven divine centers in the human heart, and as the initiate reaches each of the great initiations of Major Mysteries, he penetrates into each of these cardiac centers.
2. The initiate has access to each of these centers in each of the seven great initiations of Major Mysteries.
3. In the First Initiation of Major Mysteries, the initiate has the right to enter the first center; with the Second he enters the second; with the Third, in the third; with the Fourth, in the fourth; with the Fifth, in the fifth; with the Sixth, in the sixth; and with the Seventh, in the seventh.
4. A mount of immaculate whiteness with the figure of a pyramid is presented before you. Now, sibling, enter this sacred chamber where the image of the Crucified One shines. You have penetrated into this center before, but now you are entering into it for the fourth time, and in a very elevated form.
5. We always pass through the same centers, each time in a more elevated form, by following the curve of cosmic evolution.
6. Now, sibling of mine, enter the second center and receive your feasts and your gifts.
7. Enter the third center and make your ardent sphere that hangs from a rope to spin... Receive, sibling of mine, music and feasts.
8. Now, enter the fourth center, oh arhat, oh imperator of the cosmic mind.
9. This fourth center corresponds to the Fourth Initiation of Major Mysteries.
10. You are before the dawn of life, sibling of mine... You were a primitive, savage Indian within the virginal jungle of Arcadia... You worshipped the rising sun, yet you did

not use reasoning. You guided yourself wisely with only the voice of your instinct.

11. At the end of your journey, sibling of mine, after having Christified your mind, you found that the end is equal to the beginning plus the experience of the cycle.

12. Are you convinced that you cannot know more than God?

13. Reasoning is a crime of great magnitude against God.

14. Due to your poor rationalism, you believed that you could know more than God, but you were mistaken, sibling of mine.

15. You have now returned, sibling of mine, to the positive pole of the instinct, because the end is equal to the beginning plus the experience of the cycle.

16. You have returned to the kingdom of intuition, sibling of mine.

17. Are you now convinced of the uselessness of reasoning?

18. Only the path of straight action, ruled by the voice of silence, can take us to the heights of Nirvana.

19. Rather than using reasoning and destroying the mental body with the battle of antitheses, it is better to work intensely for the benefit of the human species.

20. When reasoning attacks you, then defeat it with the whip of willpower.

21. When the antithetic battle of concepts wants to divide your mind, throw it from you with the whip of willpower and occupy yourself with your duties, in order not to leave the field open for useless reasoning.

22. The only thing that the Lords of Karma are interested in are your works.

23. The Lords of Karma are not interested in your reasoning processes.

24. The process of conceptual selection, the depressing process of options, causes serious damage to the mental body.

25. When the damage crystallizes in the physical brain, then sicknesses of the brain appear, such as intellectual mania, alcoholism, neurasthenia, and madness.

26. You cannot know more than God, sibling of mine. Thus, your reasoning is good for nothing. Cast all the merchants out of the temple of your mind with the terrific whip of willpower.

27. Christify your mind, good disciple. Transmute the water into wine and open your doors to your internal God, so that he may teach you the divine wisdom. Thus you will eat the bread of wisdom without the necessity of useless reasoning that destroys your mental body.

28. There are hospitals and clinics in the mental plane, where millions of mentally ill bodies are confined because of the painful process of reasoning.

29. The mental bodies of many initiates that have destroyed their minds with the process of reasoning are hospitalized in these hospitals of the world of the mind.

30. The mind must flow silently and integrally without the depressing process of reasoning.

31. What is important is the path of straight action. What is important is intuitive action.

32. Intuitive action is just action, just thought, just feeling, divine transmutation, action of plenitude, complete activity, just activity, expressed sanctity, work in plenitude, wisdom in action, and active love.

33. The humanity of Aquarius will be an intuitive humanity.

34. Oh imperator, you saw how many beings began this journey with you.

35. Millions of human beings began to climb the spiral mountain of life. Yet, the majority of them tumbled into the abyss and converted themselves into demons.

36. Only a handful of beings have reached the top of the mountain with you.

37. Enter the temple, oh arhat, in order to celebrate the feast.

38. The temple is decorated for the feast.

39. Sanat Kumara, the Elder of Days, awaits for you upon his throne.

40. His majestic voice resounds as the voice of the army.

41. The Mother Goddess of the world places the sacred mantle of the buddhas and the diadem with the Eye of Shiva upon your head.
42. The Eye of Dangma shines in your middlebrow, and Sanat Kumara exclaims, "You are a buddha. You have liberated yourself from the four bodies of sin. You are an inhabitant of the world of the gods... You are a buddha."
43. The ancient of days gives you the tunic of the Buddha... Receive it, sibling of mine!
44. During these moments, a child filled with beauty comes out of your mental body. He is the psychic extraction of your mental body. He is your Christ-mind.
45. This beautiful creature is now completely fused with your divine eternal triad.
46. The Christ-mind is formed in your mental body.
47. The Christ-mind is pure, transmuted semen.
48. The Christ-mind is the result of sexual magic.
49. You are a blessed one, oh buddha!
50. Sanat Kumara offers you a new throne.
51. All the brothers and sisters of the temple are happy. All are rejoicing with the new buddha. All of them embrace you and kiss you with holy kisses.
52. The feast is immense...
53. The Mother Goddess of the world has given birth to a new buddha in the world of the gods.
54. Now you are shining with immaculate beauty within this igneous rose of nature.
55. Your inferior manas has been fused with Atman-Buddhi-Manas on the seat of pure Brahma, where only the sacred wisdom of Buddhadharma shines.
56. The Mother Goddess of the world exclaims, "Behold, here is a very beloved son. Here is a new buddha."
57. This is the wisdom of the heart. This is the seal of the heart's wisdom.
58. At last, mind and heart are totally fused.
59. The music of the spheres resounds within the divine environs and the goddesses dance with the sacred runes in the temple of the gods.

Chapter 38

Dreams and Astral Experiences

1. We finish the first part of this work by inviting all human beings to receive the direct knowledge.
2. Most students are already so separated from nature that when they talk about astral experiences, they fall into the horrible aberration of wanting to establish an abyss between astral experiences and their dreams.
3. These students despise their dream experiences, without realizing that their dreams are indeed the very astral experiences that they are looking for.
4. They fall into the same error—or similar error—of wanting to establish an abyss between clairvoyance and imagination.
5. These types of mistakes arise because the mind of the student is filled with artifices, and instead of looking for everything inside, within the realm of nature, they fall into the absurdity of looking for everything outside...
6. Thus, they erroneously believe that astral experiences are something different from their dream experiences, as artificial, extra-natural, new features, etc.
7. We invite all those students to study chapters two, four, and seven of the book of the prophet Daniel, in order for these devotees to corroborate our affirmations with the sacred scriptures.
8. Our critics cannot know more than the prophet Daniel, a pure and perfect man of God.
9. Therefore, brothers and sisters of mine, I have to inform you that astral experiences are indeed the same dream experiences that are very much despised by the "erudite" of this dark age.
10. Plato, in his book *The Republic,* "Dialogue with Socrates," said that the individual is known by his dreams.
11. Tenebrous dreams are from the abyss, and the luminous dreams are from the Light.

12. During the hours of ordinary sleep, the internal man, dressed in his astral body, leaves his physical form so that the ethereal body can repair the physical body.

13. During the vigil state, many organic residues are stored in the nervous canals that obstruct the free circulation of the vital fluids.

14. Then the ego loses control over the physical body, thus is found the necessity of withdrawing from it.

15. Thus, when the internal man withdraws, the physical body falls asleep; it enters into the dream / resting state.

16. During the hours of sleep, the thyroid gland cleans with its iodine all the nervous channels, and during this time of rest the vital body focuses on the solar magnetism, in order to vitalize the red globules that flood the sanguineous channels.

17. When the sum of leukocytes exceeds the sum of erythrocytes, it is a sign that the ethereal body is ill, and consequently or as an inevitable consequence the physical body also becomes ill.

18. After normal sleep, the ethereal body totally repairs the physical body, and the solar forces that enter by the splenic chakra pass to the solar plexus and circulate freely around the nervous channels, vitalizing all the plexuses, and regulating all organic viscera and all organic ganglia by means the vasomotor nervous system.

19. Thus, this is how after sleep, our physical body is completely repaired for the new activities of the internal ego.

20. During the hours of sleep, the ego dressed in its astral body wanders outside the physical form, occupied with the activities that are familiar to it.

21. Thus, during the hours of sleep, the evildoers execute the same evil acts that they are accustomed to.

22. During the hours of sleep, all our disciples visit the temples of mysteries and work under the direction of the White Hierarchy.

23. We test the disciples during the hours of sleep.

24. Before testing the disciples, first we awaken their consciousness, and when their consciousness gives exactly

the same note of their vigil state, then we submit them to the initiatic tests.

25. In these cases, the bodies of the disciples are sleeping, but their internal consciousness acts just as it does in the vigil state.

26. If the disciples believe in those moments that they really are in bone and flesh, much better for us, because in this way, we can test them better.

27. There are no false dream experiences; even the most absurd dreams—if they are interpreted based on the law of philosophical analogies—contain magnificent revelations.

28. During the hours of sleep, all human beings are outside their physical form, and occupied in the same activities that are familiar to them. For that reason Plato, the founder of the Mysteries of Eleusis, affirmed in his *Republic* that any individual is known through his dreams.

29. Students acquire "continuous consciousness" little by little, in accordance with their advancement; thus they become more and more familiar with the internal worlds.

30. As soon as the disciples return to the vigil state, they must practice a retrospective exercise in order to remember all the places and instructions received during the dream.

31. All those who want to differentiate between astral experiences and dream experiences are totally mistaken.

32. Let our critics study the book of the prophet Daniel from the Old Testament, so that they can realize that astral experiences and dream experiences are the same thing.

33. We, the masters of the White Universal Brotherhood, have continuous consciousness, and whether our bodies are sleeping or in a vigil state, we are always consciously working in the internal worlds, in the work of the Father.

34. Accordingly, as the disciples awaken their chakras, they will acquire continuous consciousness, which will convert them into conscious citizens of the super-sensible worlds.

35. Disciples must not talk with anybody about their astral experiences, because the incredulous people—with their negative vibrations—will destroy the wonderful petals of their chakras, and will end up damaging their powers.
36. In the beginning, the disciple must be like a sealed book.
37. Disciples who want to know, to learn how to interpret their dreams, should study chapters 37, 38, 39, 40, and 41 of the book of Genesis, and the book of the prophet Daniel.
38. It is necessary to form Jehovah within each chakra in order to awaken the consciousness.
39. In the super-sensible worlds, common and ordinary human beings walk asleep during the hours of their sleep, and after their death.
40. When our disciples make their chakras spin, they awaken their consciousness, and then during the hours of sleep they walk in the internal worlds with their awakened consciousness.
41. It is not enough to awaken the chakras, because the chakras are wide-awake in any vulgar psychic or any black magician.
42. What is important is to form the Holy Spirit in each chakra.
43. Thus, accordingly, as the disciple is forming Jehovah in each chakra, they will awaken their consciousness in the internal worlds.
44. Jehovah is formed in each chakra by intensely practicing sexual magic with our spouse.
45. Understand that sexual magic can only be practiced with our priestess/priest spouse.
46. No man can practice sexual magic with different women, because that is adultery, and whoremongers and adulterers God will judge.
47. A woman can practice sexual magic only and exclusively with her husband, and those that violate these decrees of the Holy Gnostic Church will fall inevitably into black magic.

48. However, we must know that the authentic marriage is the union of two beings in spirit, soul, and body.
49. Religious or social formulism is nothing but a requirement that we must fulfill in order to satisfy our duties with society.
50. The Lord Jehovah gives us wisdom and magical powers.
51. Consequently, we must form Jehovah in each chakra, in order to awaken the consciousness during dreams.
52. Jehovah is the Holy Spirit that must nest within each one of our chakras.
53. In these very moments in which I am finishing this book entitled *Igneous Rose*, the Solar Logos has appeared visibly before me; he is the blessed one, the divine Rabbi of Galilee, our Lord the Christ, whose divine essence we must store in our astral body in order to form the inner Christ within ourselves, thus to raise us to the Father.
54. I, Aun Weor, have remained absorbed before the sublime presence of the head of all the souls. This is how, in this way, this book was approved.

May peace be with all of humanity.

Glossary

Absolute: Abstract space; that which is without attributes or limitations. The Absolute has three aspects: the Ain, the Ain Soph, and the Ain Soph Aur.

"The Absolute is the Being of all Beings. The Absolute is that which Is, which always has Been, and which always will Be. The Absolute is expressed as Absolute Abstract Movement and Repose. The Absolute is the cause of Spirit and of Matter, but It is neither Spirit nor Matter. The Absolute is beyond the mind; the mind cannot understand It. Therefore, we have to intuitively understand Its nature." - Samael Aun Weor, *Tarot and Kabbalah*

"In the Absolute we go beyond karma and the gods, beyond the law. The mind and the individual consciousness are only good for mortifying our lives. In the Absolute we do not have an individual mind or individual consciousness; there, we are the unconditioned, free and absolutely happy Being. The Absolute is life free in its movement, without conditions, limitless, without the mortifying fear of the law, life beyond spirit and matter, beyond karma and suffering, beyond thought, word and action, beyond silence and sound, beyond forms." - Samael Aun Weor, *The Major Mysteries*

Agni: A Hindu symbol of the creative fire at the base of all things. One of the most ancient symbols in the world, representing the source and power of the sun, lightning, and fire. The Rig Veda states that all the gods are centered in Agni (fire).

"Shine thou before us, Agni, well enkindled, with flame, most youthful God, that never fadeth. [...] Seven fuel logs hast thou, seven tongues, O Agni, seven Rishis hast thou, seven beloved mansions. Seven-priests in sevenfold manner pay thee worship. Fill full—All-hail to thee!—seven wombs with butter." - White Yajurveda

There is also a great master named Agni, who is related to that root creative fire.

"Agni is the god of fire. This great master helps to restore the fire in each of the seven bodies: physical, ethereal, astral, mental, causal, buddhic, and atmic." - Samael Aun Weor, *Logos Mantra Theurgy*

Alchemy: Al (as a connotation of the Arabic word Allah: al-, the + ilah, God) means "The God." Also Al (Hebrew) for "highest" or El "God." Chem or Khem is from kimia which means "to fuse or cast a metal." Also from Khem, the ancient name of Egypt. The synthesis is Al-Kimia: "to fuse with the highest" or "to fuse with God." Alchemy is one of the oldest sciences in the world, and is the method to transmute our inner impurity into purity. It is also known in the East as Tantra.

Astral: This term is dervied from "pertaining to or proceeding from the stars," but in the esoteric knowledge it refers to the emotional aspect of the fifth dimension, which in Hebrew is called Hod.

Astral Body: What is commonly called the astral body is not the true astral body, it is rather the lunar protoplasmatic body, also known as the kama rupa (Sanskrit, "body of desires") or "dream body" (Tibetan rmi-lam-gyi lus). The true astral body is solar (being superior to lunar nature) and must be created, as the Master Jesus indicated in the Gospel of John 3:5-6, "Except a man be born of water and of the Spirit, he cannot enter into the kingdom of God. That which is born of the flesh is flesh; and that which is born of the Spirit is spirit." The solar astral body is created as a result of the Third Initiation of Major Mysteries (Serpents of Fire), and is perfected in the Third Serpent of Light. In Tibetan Buddhism, the solar astral body is known as the illusory body (sgyu-lus). This body is related to the emotional center and to the sephirah Hod.

"Really, only those who have worked with the Maithuna (White Tantra) for many years can possess the astral body." - Samael Aun Weor, *The Elimination of Satan's Tail*

Atman: (Sanskrit, literally "self") An ancient and important word that is grossly misinterpreted in much of Hinduism and Buddhism. Many have misunderstood this word as referring to a permanently existing self or soul. Yet the true meaning is otherwise.

"Brahman, Self, Purusha, Chaitanya, Consciousness, God, Atman, Immortality, Freedom, Perfection, Bliss, Bhuma or the unconditioned are synonymous terms." - Swami Sivananva

Thus, Atman as "self" refers to a state of being "unconditioned," which is related to the Absolute, the Ain Soph, or the Shunyata (Emptiness). Thus, Atman refers to the Innermost, the Spirit, the Son of God, who longs to return to that which is beyond words.

"Atman, in Himself, is the ineffable Being, the one who is beyond time and eternity, without end of days. He does not die, neither reincarnates (the ego is what returns), but Atman is absolutely perfect." - Samael Aun Weor

In general use, the term Atman can also refer to the spirit or sephirah Chesed.

"The Being Himself is Atman, the Ineffable. If we commit the error of giving the Being the qualifications of superior "I," alter ego, subliminal "I," or divine ego, etc., we commit blasphemy, because That which is Divine, the Reality, can never fall into the heresy of separability. Superior and inferior are two sections of the same thing. Superior "I" or inferior "I" are two sections of the same pluralized ego (Satan). The Being is the Being, and the reason for the Being to be is to be the same Being. The Being transcends the personality, the "I," and individuality." - Samael Aun Weor

"Bliss is the essential nature of man. The central fact of man's being is his inherent divinity. Man's essential nature is divine, the awareness of which he has lost because of his animal propensities and the veil of ignorance. Man, in his ignorance, identifies himself with the body, mind, Prana and the senses. Transcending these, he becomes one with Brahman or the Absolute who is pure bliss. Brahman or the Absolute is the fullest reality, the completest consciousness. That beyond which there is nothing, that which is the innermost Self of all is Atman or Brahman. The Atman is the common Consciousness in all beings. A thief, a prostitute, a scavenger, a king, a rogue, a saint, a dog, a cat, a rat-all have the same common Atman. There is apparent, fictitious difference in bodies and minds only. There are differences in colours and opinions. But, the Atman is the same in all. If you are very rich, you can have a steamer, a train, an airship of your own for your own selfish interests. But, you cannot have an Atman of your own. The Atman is common to all. It is not an individual's sole registered property. The Atman is the one amidst the many. It is constant amidst the forms which come and go. It is the pure, absolute, essential Consciousness of all the conscious beings. The source of all life, the source of all knowledge is the Atman, thy innermost Self. This Atman or Supreme Soul is transcendent, inexpressible, uninferable, unthinkable, indescribable, the ever-peaceful, all-blissful. There is no difference between the Atman and bliss. The Atman is bliss itself. God, perfection, peace, immortality, bliss are one. The goal of life is to attain perfection, immortality or God. The nearer one approaches the Truth, the happier one becomes. For, the essential nature of Truth is positive, absolute bliss. There is no bliss in the finite. Bliss is only in the Infinite. Eternal bliss can be had only from the eternal Self. To know the Self is to enjoy eternal bliss and everlasting peace. Self-realisation bestows eternal existence, absolute knowledge, and perennial bliss. None can be saved without Self-realisation. The quest for the Absolute should be undertaken even sacrificing the dearest object, even life, even courting all pain. Study philosophical books as much as you like, deliver lectures and lectures throughout your global tour, remain in a Himalayan cave for one hundred years, practise Pranayama for fifty years, you cannot attain emancipation without the realisation of the oneness of the Self." - Swami Sivananda

Bodhisattva: (Sanskrit; Tibetan: changchub sempa) Literally, Bodhi means "enlightenment" or "wisdom." Sattva means "essence" or "goodness," therefore the term Bodhisattva literally means "essence of wisdom." In the esoteric or secret teachings of Tibet and Gnosticism, a Bodhisattva is a human being who has reached the Fifth Initiation of Fire (Tiphereth) and has chosen to continue working by means of the Straight Path, renouncing the easier Spiral Path (in Nirvana), and returning instead to help suffering humanity. By means of this sacrifice, this individual incarnates the Christ (Avalokitesvara), thereby embodying the supreme source of wisdom and compassion. This is the entrance to the Direct Path to complete liberation from the ego, a route that only very few take, due to the fact that one must pay the entirety of one's karma in one life. Those who have taken this road have been the most remarkable figures in human history: Jesus, Buddha, Mohammed, Krishna, Moses, Padmasambhava, Milarepa, Joan of Arc, Fu-Ji, and many others whose names are not remembered or known. Of course, even among bodhisattvas there are many levels of Being: to be a bodhisattva does not mean that one is enlightened. Interestingly, the Christ in Hebrew is called Chokmah, which means "wisdom," and in Sanskrit the same is Vishnu, the root of the word "wisdom." It is Vishnu who sent his Avatars into the world in order to guide humanity. These avatars were Krishna, Buddha, Rama, and the Avatar of this age: the Avatar Kalki.

Brahmanadi: "The Brahmanadi or "canalis centralis" within which the Kundalini ascends exists throughout the length of the spinal medulla... Each one of our seven bodies has its own spinal medulla and its Brahmanadi." - Samael Aun Weor, *Kundalini Yoga*

"Within the Sushumna Nadi there is a Nadi by name Vajra. Chitra Nadi, a minute canal, which is also called Brahmanadi, is within this Vajra Nadi. Kundalini, when awakened, passes through Chitra Nadi." - Swami Sivananda, *Kundalini Yoga*

Brahmarandhra: (Sanskrit) "'Brahma-randhra' means the hole of Brahman. It is the dwelling house of the human soul. This is also known as "Dasamadvara," the tenth opening or the tenth door. The hollow place in the crown of the head known as anterior fontanelle in the new-born child is the Brahmarandhra. This is between the two parietal and occipital bones. This portion is very soft in a babe. When the child grows, it gets obliterated by the growth of the bones of the head. Brahma created the physical body and entered (Pravishat) the body to give illumination inside through this Brahmarandhra. In some of the Upanishads, it is stated like that. This is the most important part. It is very suitable for Nirguna Dhyana (abstract meditation). When the Yogi separates himself from the physical body at the time of death, this Brahmarandhra bursts open and Prana comes out through this opening (Kapala Moksha). "A hundred and one are the nerves of the heart. Of them one (Sushumna) has gone out piercing the head; going up through it, one attains immortality" (Kathopanishad)." - Swami Sivananda, *Kundalini Yoga*

Buddha: (Sanskrit) n. "awakened one, enlightened, sage, knowledge, wise one." adj. "awake, conscious, wise, intelligent, expanded."

Commonly used to refer simply to the Buddha Shakyamuni (the "founder" of Buddhism), the term Buddha is actually a title. There are a vast number of Buddhas, each at different levels of attainment. At the ultimate level, a Buddha is a being who has become totally free of suffering. The Inner Being (Hebrew: Chesed; Sanskrit: Atman) first becomes a Buddha when the Human Soul completes the work of the Fourth Initiation of Fire (related to Netzach, the mental body).

One of the Three Jewels (Tri-ratna), which are Buddha (the awakened one, our own inner Being), Dharma (the teaching he gives to perfect us), Sangha (the community of awakened masters who can help us awaken). The historical Buddha Shakyamuni is a very great master who continues to aid humanity. Nevertheless, he is not the only Buddha.

"Much has been said of the Buddhas. There is no doubt that there are Contemplation Buddhas and Manifestation Buddhas. Manifestation Buddhas are creatures who dominated the mind, who destroyed the ego, who did not let negative emotions enter their hearts, who did not create mental effigies in their own mind nor in the minds of others. Let us remember Tsong Khapa who reincarnated in Tibet; he was the Buddha Gautama previously. The Buddha of Buddha Amitabha is another thing, his true divine prototype. Amitabha is the Contemplation Buddha, and Gautama, we could say, is the Manifestation Buddha, the worldly Buddha or Bodhisattva. We cannot deny that Amitabha expressed himself brilliantly through Gautama. We cannot deny that later Amitabha sent Gautama (the Bodhisattva or worldly Buddha) directly to a new reincarnation. Then he expressed himself as Tsong Khapa. These are Contemplation Buddhas, they are masters of their mind, creatures who liberated themselves from the mind. The Lords worship the Great Buddha that we also know as the Logos and they pray to him." - Samael Aun Weor from the lecture entitled Mental Representations

"We know very well that Atman-Buddhi is the Inner Buddha, the Buddha, the Innermost; this is how it is written in the Sanskrit books. Now then, we know that Christ is the Second Logos; since the First Logos is Brahma, the Second is Vishnu (the Son) and Shiva is the Third Logos (the Holy Spirit). Therefore, the Inner Christ, evidently and within the levels of the Being, or better said, within the levels of our Superlative and Transcendental Being, is beyond our Inner Buddha, yet they complement each other. Two types of Buddhas exist; yes, we know this. There exist the Transitory Buddhas and the Permanent Buddhas. A Transitory Buddha is a Buddha who still has not achieved within himself the incarnation of the Inner Christ. A Permanent Buddha or Buddha of Contemplation is a Buddha who has already Christified himself, a Buddha that has already received the Inner Christ within his own internal nature. This type of Buddha is a Buddha Maitreya, since it is a Buddha who incarnated the Inner Christ (this is how the term "Maitreya" should be understood). So, Buddha Maitreya is not a person: Buddha Maitreya is a title, a degree, which indicates any given Buddha who already achieved Christification." - The Esoteric Path

"The Buddha appears in the world so that sentient beings may obtain the gnosis that he himself obtained. Thus, the Buddha's demonstrations of the path are strictly means to lead sentient beings to buddhahood." - The Fourteenth Dalai Lama [http://www.dalailama.com/page.22.htm]

Buddhi: (Sanskrit, literally "intelligence") An aspect of mind.

"Buddhi is pure [superior] reason. The seat of Buddhi is just below the crown of the head in the Pineal Gland of the brain. Buddhi is manifested only in those persons who have developed right intuitive discrimination or Viveka. The ordinary reason of the worldly people is termed practical reason, which is dense and has limitations... Sankhya Buddhi or Buddhi in the light of Sankhya philosophy is will and intellect combined. Mind is microcosm. Mind is Maya. Mind occupies an intermediate state between Prakriti and Purusha, matter and Spirit." - Swami Sivananda, *Yoga in Daily Life*

"When the diverse, confining sheaths of the Atma have been dissolved by Sadhana, when the different Vrittis of the mind have been controlled by mental drill or gymnastic, when the conscious mind is not active, you enter the realm of spirit life, the super-conscious mind where Buddhi and pure reason and intuition, the faculty of direct cognition of Truth, manifest. You pass into the kingdom of peace where there is none to speak, you will hear the voice of God which is very clear and pure and has an upward tendency. Listen to the voice with attention and interest. It will guide you. It is the voice of God." - Swami Sivananda, *Essence of Yoga*

In Kabbalah: The feminine Spiritual Soul, related to the sephirah Geburah. Symbolized throughout world literature, notably as Helen of Troy, Beatrice in The Divine Comedy, and Beth-sheba (Hebrew, literally "daughter of seven") in the Old Testament. The Divine or Spiritual Soul is the feminine soul of the Innermost (Atman), or his "daughter." All the strength, all the power of the Gods and Goddesses resides in Buddhi / Geburah, Cosmic Consciousness, as within a glass of alabaster where the flame of the Inner Being (Gedulah, Atman the Ineffable) is always burning. Centers: The human being has seven centers of psychological activity. The first five are the Intellectual, Emotional, Motor, Instinctive, and Sexual Centers. However, through inner development one learns how to utilize the Superior Emotional and Superior Intellectual Centers. Most people do not use these two at all.

The seven centers are also referred to as three centers: Intellectual, Emotional, and Motor-Instinctive-Sexual.

Chaos: (Greek) There are three primary applications of this term.

"The first Chaos from which the cosmos emerged is between the Sephiroth Binah and Chesed. The second Chaos, from where the fundamental principles of the human being emerged, exists within Yesod-Mercury, which is the sexual human center. The third Chaos, the Infernal Worlds, exists below the Thirteenth Aeons in the region of Klipoth, in the underworld." - Samael Aun Weor, *The Gnostic Bible: The Pistis Sophia Unveiled*

The Abyss (not the Inferior Abyss), or the "Great Deep." Personified as the Egyptian Goddess Neith. The Great Mother, the Immaculate Virgin from which arises all matter. The Chaos is WITHIN the Ain Soph. The primitive state of the universe. Esoterically, a reference to the semen, both in the microcosm and the macrocosm. Alchemically, it is said to be a mixture of water & fire, and it holds the seeds of the cosmos.

Chakra: (Sanskrit) Literally, "wheel." The chakras are subtle centers of energetic transformation. There are hundreds of chakras in our hidden physiology, but seven primary ones related to the awakening of consciousness.

"The Chakras are centres of Shakti as vital force... The Chakras are not perceptible to the gross senses. Even if they were perceptible in the living body which they help to organise, they disappear with the disintegration of organism at death." - Swami Sivananda, *Kundalini Yoga*

"The chakras are points of connection through which the divine energy circulates from one to another vehicle of the human being." - Samael Aun Weor, *Aztec Christic Magic*

Chastity: Although modern usage has rendered the term chastity virtually meaningless to most people, its original meaning and usage clearly indicate "moral purity" upon the basis of "sexual purity." Contemporary usage implies "repression" or "abstinence," which have nothing to do with real chastity. True chastity is a rejection of impure sexuality. True chastity is pure sexuality, or the activity of sex in harmony with our true nature, as explained in the secret doctrine. Properly used, the word chastity refers to sexual fidelity or honor.

"The generative energy, which, when we are loose, dissipates and makes us unclean, when we are continent invigorates and inspires us. Chastity is the flowering of man; and what are called Genius, Heroism, Holiness, and the like, are but various fruits which succeed it." - Henry David Thoreau, *Walden*

Christ: Derived from the Greek Christos, "the Anointed One," and Krestos, whose esoteric meaning is "fire." The word Christ is a title, not a personal name.

"Indeed, Christ is a Sephirothic Crown (Kether, Chokmah and Binah) of incommensurable wisdom, whose purest atoms shine within Chokmah, the world of the Ophanim. Christ is not the Monad, Christ is not the Theosophical Septenary; Christ is not the Jivan-Atman. Christ is the Central Sun. Christ is the ray that unites us to the Absolute." - Samael Aun Weor, *Tarot and Kabbalah*

"The Gnostic Church adores the saviour of the world, Jesus. The Gnostic Church knows that Jesus incarnated Christ, and that is why they adore him. Christ is not a human nor a divine individual. Christ is a title given to all fully self-realized masters. Christ is the Army of the Voice. Christ is the Verb. The Verb is far beyond the body, the soul and the Spirit. Everyone who is able to incarnate the Verb receives in fact the title of Christ. Christ is the Verb itself. It is necessary for everyone of us to incarnate the Verb (Word). When the Verb becomes flesh in us we speak with the verb of light. In actuality, several masters have incarnated the Christ. In secret India, the Christ Yogi Babaji has lived for millions of years; Babaji is immortal. The great master of wisdom Kout Humi also incarnated the Christ. Sanat

Kumara, the founder of the great College of Initiates of the White Lodge, is another living Christ. In the past, many incarnated the Christ. In the present, some have incarnated the Christ. In the future many will incarnate the Christ. John the Baptist also incarnated the Christ. John the Baptist is a living Christ. The difference between Jesus and the other masters that also incarnated the Christ has to do with hierarchy. Jesus is the highest Solar initiate of the cosmos..." - Samael Aun Weor, *The Perfect Matrimony*

Clairvoyance: A term invented by occultists, derived from the French clair "clear," and voyance "seeing."

"There exist clairvoyance and pseudo-clairvoyance. The Gnostic student must make a clear differentiation between these two forms of extrasensory perception. Clairvoyance is based on objectivity. However, pseudo-clairvoyance is based on subjectivity. Understand that by objectivity we mean spiritual reality, the spiritual world. Understand that by subjectivity we mean the physical world, the world of illusion, that which has no reality. An intermediate region also exists, this is the astral world, which can be objective or subjective according to the degree of spiritual development of each person." - Samael Aun Weor, *The Perfect Matrimony*

"Positive clairvoyance is achieved only with a great intellectual culture and a great esoteric discipline. The highest cultured people, who are submitted to the most rigorous intellectual disciplines, only achieve the truly positive clairvoyance. The illuminated intellect is the outcome of positive clairvoyance." - Samael Aun Weor, *Fundamental Notions of Endocrinology and Criminology*

The two main categories of consciousness are objective (positive, related with free consciousness) and subjective (negative, related to the deluded perception and opinions of the psychological "I"s). Further, there are five types of clairvoyance, as explained in *Fundamental Notions of Endocrinology and Criminology.*

1. Conscious clairvoyance: to perceive any given phenomenon (whether internal phenomenon related with the psyche and internal worlds or external phenomenon related to the circumstances of the physical world and nature) through the intelligence of the Monad which is essence or consciousness. Conscious clairvoyance is experienced when one is able to perceive a physical or psychological phenomenon how it really is, in all of its causes and multiple dimensions.

2. Supra-conscious clairvoyance: This is the level of Logoic consciousness. This is only for those venerable masters who finish The Great Work. This level of consciousness is Turiya, those masters who have no ego, who have resurrected, and for those who never dream.

3. Subconscious clairvoyance: This is related to the perception of the egos who are related with memories of past experience. These egos are the most superficial egos whose inherent pattern was defined during the formation of the personality (birth to seven years old). These egos can be created at any time in our lives but the pattern is related to the false personality and

the PCPF. An example of a subconscious ego is the one who avoids broccoli for their entire lives because they remember the disgust they had when they were forced to eat it by their parents. Remember that subconscious clairvoyance is the way the ego perceives that particular experience; as in the example, it was the way the ego perceives the impression of broccoli and that example.

4. Unconscious clairvoyance: This is the type of perception that develops through the frustration of desires. Pride constantly talks about himself and how great he is because it if frustrated that nobody else talks about him; this is an unconscious habit. Lust becomes frustrated because it was never able to satisfy its sexual desire to fornicate with a particular movie star, etc. This desire becomes frustrated and in the astral plane projects its frustrated desires in the form of sexual dreams with the image/impression of the movie star.

5. Infra-conscious clairvoyance: The deepest aspects of our egos, related to the spheres of Lilith in the Klipoth. Remember that everything in the universe has its antithesis. The antithesis of the angel of love, Anael, is Lilith, the demon of fornication, black magic and homosexuality. This region is usually only experienced during nightmares. A minority of people bring these egos to the surface, incorporating these elements in action and with the personality. Sadly, this humanity has more and more people who bring the elements of black magic, homosexuality and brutality to the surface of their psychological world.

Consciousness: "Wherever there is life, there is consciousness. Consciousness is inherent to life as humidity is inherent to water." - Samael Aun Weor, *Fundamental Notions of Endocrinology and Criminology*

From various dictionaries: 1. The state of being conscious; knowledge of one's own existence, condition, sensations, mental operations, acts, etc. 2. Immediate knowledge or perception of the presence of any object, state, or sensation. 3. An alert cognitive state in which you are aware of yourself and your situation. In universal Gnosticism, the range of potential consciousness is allegorized in the Ladder of Jacob, upon which the angels ascend and descend. Thus there are higher and lower levels of consciousness, from the level of demons at the bottom, to highly realized angels in the heights.

"It is vital to understand and develop the conviction that consciousness has the potential to increase to an infinite degree." - The 14th Dalai Lama

"Light and consciousness are two phenomena of the same thing; to a lesser degree of consciousness, corresponds a lesser degree of light; to a greater degree of consciousness, a greater degree of light." - Samael Aun Weor, *The Esoteric Treatise of Hermetic Astrology*

Devic path: "...when arriving at the degree of Aseka, or hierophant of the Fifth Initiation of Major Mysteries, the following seven paths are opened before the master:

a) To continue with humanity, working for humanity.

b) To continue within the internal planes as Nirmanakaya, working for humanity.

c) To join the evolution of the angels or devas.

d) To form part of the government of the Logos.

e) To prepare the work of the future Ethereal Age of the Earth.

f) To enter into the ineffable joy of Nirvana.

g) To perform superior works of Nirvana." - Samael Aun Weor, *Esoteric Medicine and Practical Magic*

Divine Mother: "Among the Aztecs, she was known as Tonantzin, among the Greeks as chaste Diana. In Egypt she was Isis, the Divine Mother, whose veil no mortal has lifted. There is no doubt at all that esoteric Christianity has never forsaken the worship of the Divine Mother Kundalini. Obviously she is Marah, or better said, RAM-IO, MARY. What orthodox religions did not specify, at least with regard to the exoteric or public circle, is the aspect of Isis in her individual human form. Clearly, it was taught only in secret to the Initiates that this Divine Mother exists individually within each human being. It cannot be emphasized enough that Mother-God, Rhea, Cybele, Adonia, or whatever we wish to call her, is a variant of our own individual Being in the here and now. Stated explicitly, each of us has our own particular, individual Divine Mother." - Samael Aun Weor, *The Great Rebellion*

"Devi Kundalini, the Consecrated Queen of Shiva, our personal Divine Cosmic Individual Mother, assumes five transcendental mystic aspects in every creature, which we must enumerate:

1. The unmanifested Prakriti

2. The chaste Diana, Isis, Tonantzin, Maria or better said Ram-Io

3. The terrible Hecate, Persephone, Coatlicue, queen of the infemos and death; terror of love and law

4. The special individual Mother Nature, creator and architect of our physical organism

5. The Elemental Enchantress to whom we owe every vital impulse, every instinct." - Samael Aun Weor, *The Mystery of the Golden Blossom*

Ego: The multiplicity of contradictory psychological elements that we have inside are in their sum the "ego." Each one is also called "an ego" or an "I." Every ego is a psychological defect which produces suffering. The ego is three (related to our Three Brains or three centers of psychological processing), seven (capital sins), and legion (in their infinite variations).

"The ego is the root of ignorance and pain." - Samael Aun Weor, *The Esoteric Treatise of Hermetic Astrology*

"The Being and the ego are incompatible. The Being and the ego are like water and oil. They can never be mixed... The annihilation of the psychic aggregates (egos) can be made possible only by radically comprehending our errors through meditation and by the evident Self-reflection of the Being." - Samael Aun Weor, *The Gnostic Bible: The Pistis Sophia Unveiled*

Elemental: The intelligence or soul of all creatures below the Human Kingdom, whose physical bodies are the minerals, plants and animals, but whose souls are gnomes, sprites, elves and fairies. (Strictly speaking, even Intellectual Animals remain as elementals until they create the soul; however in common usage the term elementals refers to the creatures of the three lower kingdoms: mineral, plant, and animal).

"In the times of King Arthur and the Knights of the Round Table, elementals of Nature were manifest everywhere, deeply penetrating our physical atmosphere. Many are the tales of elves, leprechauns and fairies, which still abound in green Erin, Ireland. Unfortunately, all these things of innocence, all this beauty from the soul of the Earth, is no longer perceived by humanity. This is due to the intellectual scoundrel's pedantries and the animal ego's excessive development." - Samael Aun Weor, *The Great Rebellion*

Fohat: (Theosophical/Tibetan) A term used by H.P. Blavatsky to represent the active (male) potency of the Shakti (female sexual power) in nature, the essence of cosmic electricity, vital force. As explained in *The Secret Doctrine*, "He (Fohat) is, metaphysically, the objectivised thought of the gods; the "Word made flesh" on a lower scale, and the messenger of Cosmic and human ideations: the active force in Universal Life.... In India, Fohat is connected with Vishnu and Surya in the early character of the (first) God; for Vishnu is not a high god in the Rig Veda. The name Vishnu is from the root vish, "to pervade," and Fohat is called the "Pervader" and the Manufacturer, because he shapes the atoms from crude material..." The term fohat has recently been linked with the Tibetan verb phro-wa and the noun spros-pa. These two terms are listed in Jäschke's Tibetan-English Dictionary (1881) as, for phro-wa, "to proceed, issue, emanate from, to spread, in most cases from rays of light..." while for spros-pa he gives "business, employment, activity."

Fornication: Originally, the term fornication was derived from the Indo-European word gwher, whose meanings relate to heat and burning (the full explanation can be found online at http://sacred-sex.org/terminology/fornication). Fornication means to make the heat (solar fire) of the seed (sexual power) leave the body through voluntary orgasm. Any voluntary orgasm is fornication, whether between a married man and woman, or an unmarried man and woman, or through masturbation, or in any other case; this is explained by Moses: "A man from whom there is a discharge of semen, shall immerse all his flesh in water, and he shall remain unclean until evening. And any garment or any leather [object] which has semen on it, shall be immersed in water, and shall remain unclean until evening. A woman with whom a man cohabits, whereby there was [a discharge of] semen, they shall immerse in water, and they shall remain unclean until evening." - Leviticus 15:16-18

To fornicate is to spill the sexual energy through the orgasm. Those who "deny themselves" restrain the sexual energy, and "walk in the midst of the fire" without being burned. Those who restrain the sexual energy, who renounce the orgasm, remember God in themselves, and do not defile themselves with animal passion, "for the temple of God is holy, which temple ye are."

"Whosoever is born of God doth not commit sin; for his seed remaineth in him: and he cannot sin, because he is born of God." - 1 John 3:9

This is why neophytes always took a vow of sexual abstention, so that they could prepare themselves for marriage, in which they would have sexual relations but not release the sexual energy through the orgasm. This is why Paul advised:

"...they that have wives be as though they had none..." - I Corinthians 7:29

"A fornicator is an individual who has intensely accustomed his genital organs to copulate (with orgasm). Yet, if the same individual changes his custom of copulation to the custom of no copulation, then he transforms himself into a chaste person. We have as an example the astonishing case of Mary Magdalene, who was a famous prostitute. Mary Magdalene became the famous Saint Mary Magdalene, the repented prostitute. Mary Magdalene became the chaste disciple of Christ." - Samael Aun Weor, *The Revolution of Beelzebub*

Gnosis: (Greek) Knowledge.

1. The word Gnosis refers to the knowledge we acquire through our own experience, as opposed to knowledge that we are told or believe in. Gnosis - by whatever name in history or culture - is conscious, experiential knowledge, not merely intellectual or conceptual knowledge, belief, or theory. This term is synonymous with the Hebrew "daath" and the Sanskrit "jna."

2. The tradition that embodies the core wisdom or knowledge of humanity.

"Gnosis is the flame from which all religions sprouted, because in its depth Gnosis is religion. The word "religion" comes from the Latin word "religare," which implies "to link the Soul to God"; so Gnosis is the very pure flame from where all religions sprout, because Gnosis is knowledge, Gnosis is wisdom." - Samael Aun Weor from the lecture entitled The Esoteric Path

"The secret science of the Sufis and of the Whirling Dervishes is within Gnosis. The secret doctrine of Buddhism and of Taoism is within Gnosis. The sacred magic of the Nordics is within Gnosis. The wisdom of Hermes, Buddha, Confucius, Mohammed and Quetzalcoatl, etc., etc., is within Gnosis. Gnosis is the doctrine of Christ." - Samael Aun Weor, *The Revolution of Beelzebub*

Holy Spirit: The Christian name for the third aspect of the Holy Trinity, or "God." This force has other names in other religions. In Kabbalah, the third sephirah, Binah. In Buddhism, it is related to Nirmanakaya, the "body of formation" through which the inner Buddha works in the world.

"The Holy Spirit is the Fire of Pentecost or the fire of the Holy Spirit called Kundalini by the Hindus, the igneous serpent of our magical powers, Holy Fire symbolized by Gold..." - Samael Aun Weor, *The Perfect Matrimony*

"It has been said in The Divine Comedy with complete clarity that the Holy Spirit is the husband of the Divine Mother. Therefore, the Holy Spirit unfolds himself into his wife, into the Shakti of the Hindus. This must be known and understood. Some, when they see that the Third Logos is unfolded into the Divine Mother Kundalini, or Shakti, She that has many names, have believed that the Holy Spirit is feminine, and they have been mistaken. The Holy Spirit is masculine, but when He unfolds Himself into She, then the first ineffable Divine Couple is formed, the Creator Elohim, the Kabir, or Great Priest, the Ruach Elohim, that in accordance to Moses, cultivated the waters in the beginning of the world." - Samael Aun Weor, *Tarot and Kabbalah*

"The Primitive Gnostic Christians worshipped the lamb, the fish and the white dove as symbols of the Holy Spirit." - Samael Aun Weor, *The Perfect Matrimony*

Initiation: The process whereby the Innermost (the Inner Father) receives recognition, empowerment and greater responsibilities in the Internal Worlds, and little by little approaches His goal: complete Self-realization, or in other words, the return into the Absolute. Initiation NEVER applies to the "I" or our terrestrial personality.

"There are Nine Initiations of Minor Mysteries and seven great Initiations of Major Mysteries. The Innermost is the one who receives all of these Initiations. The Testament of Wisdom says: "Before the dawning of the false aurora upon the earth, the ones who survived the hurricane and the tempest were praising the Innermost, and the heralds of the aurora appeared unto them." The psychological "I" does not receives Initiations. The human personality does not receive anything. Nonetheless, the "I" of some Initiates becomes filled with pride when saying 'I am a Master, I have such Initiations.' Thus, this is how the "I" believes itself to be an Initiate and keeps reincarnating in order to "perfect itself", but, the "I" never ever perfects itself. The "I" only reincarnates in order to satisfy desires. That is all." - Samael Aun Weor, *The Aquarian Message*

Innermost: "Our real Being is of a universal nature. Our real Being is neither a kind of superior nor inferior "I." Our real Being is impersonal, universal, divine. He transcends every concept of "I," me, myself, ego, etc., etc." - Samael Aun Weor, *The Perfect Matrimony*

Also known as Atman, the Spirit, Chesed, our own individual interior divine Father.

"The Innermost is the ardent flame of Horeb. In accordance with Moses, the Innermost is the Ruach Elohim (the Spirit of God) who sowed the waters in the beginning of the world. He is the Sun King, our Divine Monad, the Alter-Ego of Cicerone." - Samael Aun Weor, *The Revolution of Beelzebub*

Intellectual Animal: When the Intelligent Principle, the Monad, sends its spark of consciousness into Nature, that spark, the anima, enters into manifestation as a simple mineral. Gradually, over millions of years, the anima gathers experience and evolves up the chain of life until it perfects itself in the level of the mineral kingdom. It then graduates into the plant kingdom, and subsequently into the animal kingdom. With each ascension the spark receives new capacities and higher grades of complexity. In the animal kingdom it learns procreation by ejaculation. When that animal intelligence enters into the human kingdom, it receives a new capacity: reasoning, the intellect; it is now an anima with intellect: an Intellectual Animal. That spark must then perfect itself in the human kingdom in order to become a complete and perfect human being, an entity that has conquered and transcended everything that belongs to the lower kingdoms. Unfortunately, very few intellectual animals perfect themselves; most remain enslaved by their animal nature, and thus are reabsorbed by Nature, a process belonging to the devolving side of life and called by all the great religions "Hell" or the Second Death.

"The present manlike being is not yet human; he is merely an intellectual animal. It is a very grave error to call the legion of the "I" the "soul." In fact, what the manlike being has is the psychic material, the material for the soul within his Essence, but indeed, he does not have a Soul yet." - Samael Aun Weor, *The Revolution of the Dialectic*

Internal Worlds: The many dimensions beyond the physical world. These dimensions are both subjective and objective. To know the objective internal worlds (the astral plane, or Nirvana, or the Klipoth) one must first know one's own personal, subjective internal worlds, because the two are intimately associated.

"Whosoever truly wants to know the internal worlds of the planet Earth or of the solar system or of the galaxy in which we live, must previously know his intimate world, his individual, internal life, his own internal worlds. Man, know thyself, and thou wilt know the universe and its gods. The more we explore this internal world called "myself," the more we will comprehend that we simultaneously live in two worlds, in two realities, in two confines: the external and the internal. In the same way that it is indispensable for one to learn how to walk in the external world so as not to fall down into a precipice, or not get lost in the streets of the city, or to select one's friends, or not associate with the perverse ones, or not eat poison, etc.; likewise, through the psychological work upon oneself we learn how to walk in the internal world, which is explorable only through Self-observation." - Samael Aun Weor, *Treatise of Revolutionary Psychology*

Through the work in Self-observation, we develop the capacity to awaken where previously we were asleep: including in the objective internal worlds.

Kabbalah: (Hebrew קבלה) Alternatively spelled Cabala, Qabalah from the Hebrew קבל KBLH or QBL, "to receive." An ancient esoteric teaching hidden from the uninitiated, whose branches and many forms have reached throughout the world. The true Kabbalah is the science and language of the superior worlds and is thus objective, complete and without flaw; it is said that "All enlightened beings agree," and their natural agreement is a function of the awakened consciousness. The Kabbalah is the language of that consciousness, thus disagreement regarding its meaning and interpretation is always due to the subjective elements in the psyche.

"The objective of studying the Kabbalah is to be skilled for work in the internal worlds... One that does not comprehend remains confused in the internal worlds. Kabbalah is the basis in order to understand the language of these worlds." - Samael Aun Weor, *Tarot and Kabbalah*

"In Kabbalah we have to constantly look at the Hebrew letters." - Samael Aun Weor, *Tarot and Kabbalah*

Karma: (Sanskrit, literally "deed"; derived from kri, "to do, make, cause, effect.") Causality, the Law of Cause and Effect.

"Be not deceived; God is not mocked: for whatsoever a man soweth, that shall he also reap." - Galatians 6:7

"Buddha said there are three eternal things in life: 1. The Law (Karma), 2. Nirvana, 3. Space." - Samael Aun Weor, *Tarot and Kabbalah*

Kundalini: "Kundalini, the serpent power or mystic fire, is the primordial energy or Sakti that lies dormant or sleeping in the Muladhara Chakra, the centre of the body. It is called the serpentine or annular power on account of serpentine form. It is an electric fiery occult power, the great pristine force which underlies all organic and inorganic matter. Kundalini is the cosmic power in individual bodies. It is not a material force like electricity, magnetism, centripetal or centrifugal force. It is a spiritual potential Sakti or cosmic power. In reality it has no form. [...] O Divine Mother Kundalini, the Divine Cosmic Energy that is hidden in men! Thou art Kali, Durga, Adisakti, Rajarajeswari, Tripurasundari, Maha-Lakshmi, Maha-Sarasvati! Thou hast put on all these names and forms. Thou hast manifested as Prana, electricity, force, magnetism, cohesion, gravitation in this universe. This whole universe rests in Thy bosom. Crores of salutations unto thee. O Mother of this world! Lead me on to open the Sushumna Nadi and take Thee along the Chakras to Sahasrara Chakra and to merge myself in Thee and Thy consort, Lord Siva. Kundalini Yoga is that Yoga which treats of Kundalini Sakti, the six centres of spiritual energy (Shat Chakras), the arousing of the sleeping Kundalini Sakti and its union with Lord Siva in Sahasrara Chakra, at the crown of the head. This is an exact science. This is also known as Laya Yoga. The six centres are pierced (Chakra Bheda) by the passing of Kundalini Sakti to the top of the head. 'Kundala' means 'coiled'. Her form is like a coiled serpent. Hence the name Kundalini." - Swami Sivananda, *Kundalini Yoga*

"Kundalini is a compound word: Kunda reminds us of the abominable "Kundabuffer organ," and lini is an Atlantean term meaning termination. Kundalini means "the termination of the abominable Kundabuffer organ." In this case, it is imperative not to confuse Kundalini with Kundabuffer." - Samael Aun Weor, *The Great Rebellion*

These two forces, one positive and ascending, and one negative and descending, are symbolized in the Bible in the book of Numbers (the story of the Serpent of Brass). The Kundalini is "The power of life."- from the Theosophical Glossary. The Sexual Fire that is at the base of all life.

"The ascent of the Kundalini along the spinal cord is achieved very slowly in accordance with the merits of the heart. The fires of the heart control the miraculous development of the Sacred Serpent. Devi Kundalini is not something mechanical as many suppose; the Igneous Serpent is only awakened with genuine Love between husband and wife, and it will never rise up along the medullar canal of adulterers." - Samael Aun Weor, *The Mystery of the Golden Blossom*

"The decisive factor in the progress, development and evolution of the Kundalini is ethics." - Samael Aun Weor, *The Revolution of Beelzebub*

"Until not too long ago, the majority of spiritualists believed that on awakening the Kundalini, the latter instantaneously rose to the head and the initiate was automatically united with his Innermost or Internal God, instantly, and converted into Mahatma. How comfortable! How comfortably all these theosophists, Rosicrucians and spiritualists, etc., imagined High Initiation." - Samael Aun Weor, *The Zodiacal Course*

"There are seven bodies of the Being. Each body has its "cerebrospinal" nervous system, its medulla and Kundalini. Each body is a complete organism. There are, therefore, seven bodies, seven medullae and seven Kundalinis. The ascension of each of the seven Kundalinis is slow and difficult. Each canyon or vertebra represents determined occult powers and this is why the conquest of each canyon undergoes terrible tests." - Samael Aun Weor, *The Zodiacal Course*

Logos: (Greek) means Verb or Word. In Greek and Hebrew metaphysics, the unifying principle of the world. The Logos is the manifested deity of every nation and people; the outward expression or the effect of the cause which is ever concealed. (Speech is the "logos" of thought). The Logos has three aspects, known universally as the Trinity or Trimurti. The First Logos is the Father, Brahma. The Second Logos is the Son, Vishnu. The Third Logos is the Holy Spirit, Shiva. One who incarnates the Logos becomes a Logos.

"The Logos is not an individual. The Logos is an army of ineffable beings." - Samael Aun Weor, *Fundamental Notions of Endocrinology & Criminology*

Magic: The word magic is derived from the ancient word "mag" that means priest. Real magic is the work of a priest. A real magician is a priest.

"Magic, according to Novalis, is the art of influencing the inner world consciously." - Samael Aun Weor, *The Mystery of the Golden Blossom*

"When magic is explained as it really is, it seems to make no sense to fa-
natical people. They prefer to follow their world of illusions." - Samael Aun
Weor, *The Revolution of Beelzebub*

Manas: (Sanskrit) In general use, "mind." However, in Sanskrit the word
manas can mean "imagination, intellect, inclination, will, excogitation,
temper, understanding, intention, mind, spirit or spiritual principle,
mood, perception, opinion, intelligence, breath or living soul which
escapes from the body at death, desire, sense, reflection, thought, affec-
tion, conscience, invention, spirit."

Manas is derived from the Sanskrit root man, "to think." Manas is the
root of the English term "man."

In Hinduism, the word manas is used with great flexibility and range,
and thus can be applied in a variety of ways in the understanding of our
psyche. In most cases it refers to the undisciplined mind of the common
person, that is ruled by desires and ignorant of the true nature of the self
(Atman). Manas is understood as the capacity for thought, which is one
aspect of the antahkarana, the "inner organ."

The Vedas posit two forms of manas:

buddhi manas

kama manas

The Upanishads also present two forms of manas:

"Manas (mind) is said to be of two kinds, the pure and the impure. That
which is associated with the thought of desire is the impure, while that
which is without desire is the pure. To men, their mind alone is the cause
of bondage or emancipation. That mind which is attracted by objects
of sense tends to bondage, while that which is not so attracted tends to
emancipation." - Amritabindu Upanishad

"Suddha Manas or Sattvic mind (pure mind) and Asuddha (impure)
Manas or the instinctive mind or desire-mind as it is called are the two
kinds of mind according to Upanishadic teaching. There is the lower
mind filled with passion. There is the higher mind filled with Sattva
(purity). There are two minds. You will have to make it into one — Sattvic
mind only — if you want to meditate. It is through the higher or Sattvic
mind that you will have to control the lower or instinctive mind of passions and emotions." - Swami Sivananda

In Buddhism, manas is used to refer to "mind" or "intelligence," in terms
of mental function and activity.

Samael Aun Weor uses the term manas primarily in two ways:

Superior Manas: the Human Soul, the Causal Body, the sephirah
Tiphereth

Inferior Manas: the intellect, the mental body, the sephirah Netzach

Mantra: (Sanskrit, literally "mind protection") A sacred word or sound. The
use of sacred words and sounds is universal throughout all religions and

mystical traditions, because the root of all creation is in the Great Breath or the Word, the Logos. "In the beginning was the Word..."

Meditation: "When the esotericist submerges himself into meditation, what he seeks is information." - Samael Aun Weor

"It is urgent to know how to meditate in order to comprehend any psychic aggregate, or in other words, any psychological defect. It is indispensable to know how to work with all our heart and with all our soul, if we want the elimination to occur." - Samael Aun Weor, *The Gnostic Bible: The Pistis Sophia Unveiled*

"1. The Gnostic must first attain the ability to stop the course of his thoughts, the capacity to not think. Indeed, only the one who achieves that capacity will hear the Voice of the Silence.

"2. When the Gnostic disciple attains the capacity to not think, then he must learn to concentrate his thoughts on only one thing.

"3. The third step is correct meditation. This brings the first flashes of the new consciousness into the mind.

"4. The fourth step is contemplation, ecstasy or Samadhi. This is the state of Turiya (perfect clairvoyance). - Samael Aun Weor, *The Perfect Matrimony*

Mental Body: One of the seven bodies of the human being. Related to Netzach, the seventh sephirah of the Tree of Life; corresponds to the fifth dimension. In Egyptian mysticism, it is called Ba. In Hinduism, is it called vijnanmayakosha or kama manas (some Hindu teachers think the mental body is "manomayakosha," but that is the astral body).

"The mental body is a material organism, yet it is not the physical organism. The mental body has its ultra-biology and its internal pathology, which is completely unknown to the present men of science." - Samael Aun Weor, *The Revolution of Beelzebub*

Monad: (Latin) From monas, "unity; a unit, monad." The Monad is the Being, the Innermost, our own inner Spirit.

"We must distinguish between Monads and Souls. A Monad, in other words, a Spirit, is; a Soul is acquired. Distinguish between the Monad of a world and the Soul of a world; between the Monad of a human and the Soul of a human; between the Monad of an ant and the Soul of an ant. The human organism, in final synthesis, is constituted by billions and trillions of infinitesimal Monads. There are several types and orders of primary elements of all existence, of every organism, in the manner of germs of all the phenomena of nature; we can call the latter Monads, employing the term of Leibnitz, in the absence of a more descriptive term to indicate the simplicity of the simplest existence. An atom, as a vehicle of action, corresponds to each of these genii or Monads. The Monads attract each other, combine, transform themselves, giving form to every organism, world, micro-organism, etc. Hierarchies exist among the Monads; the Inferior Monads must obey the Superior ones that is the Law. Inferior Monads belong to the Superior ones. All the trillions of Monads that animate the human organism have to obey the owner, the chief, the Principal Monad. The regulating Monad, the Primordial Monad permits the activity of all of its subordinates inside the human organism, until the time indicated by the Law of Karma." - Samael Aun Weor, *The Esoteric Treatise of Hermetic Astrology*

"(The number) one is the Monad, the Unity, Iod-Heve or Jehovah, the Father who is in secret. It is the Divine Triad that is not incarnated within a Master who has not killed the ego. He is Osiris, the same God, the Word." - Samael Aun Weor, *Tarot and Kabbalah*

"When spoken of, the Monad is referred to as Osiris. He is the one who has to Self-realize Himself... Our own particular Monad needs us and we need it. Once, while speaking with my Monad, my Monad told me, 'I am self-realizing Thee; what I am doing, I am doing for Thee.' Otherwise, why are we living? The Monad wants to Self-realize and that is why we are here. This is our objective." - Samael Aun Weor, *Tarot and Kabbalah*

"The Monads or vital genii are not exclusive to the physical organism; within the atoms of the Internal Bodies there are found imprisoned many orders and categories of living Monads. The existence of any physical or supersensible, Angelic or Diabolical, Solar or Lunar body, has billions and trillions of Monads as their foundation." - Samael Aun Weor, *The Esoteric Treatise of Hermetic Astrology* Ninth **Sphere:** In Kabbalah, a reference to the sephirah Yesod of the Tree of Life (Kabbalah). When you place the Tree of Life over your body, you see that Yesod is related to your sexual organs.

"The Ninth Sphere of the Kabbalah is sex." - Samael Aun Weor, *The Perfect Matrimony*

The Ninth Sphere also refers to the sephirah Yesod and to the lowest sphere of the Klipoth.

"The great Master Hilarion IX said that in ancient times, to descend into the Ninth Sphere was the maximum ordeal for the supreme dignity of the Hierophant. Hermes, Buddha, Jesus Christ, Dante, Zoroaster, Mohammed, Rama, Krishna, Pythagoras, Plato and many others, had to descend into the Ninth Sphere in order to work with the fire and the water which is the origin of worlds, beasts, human beings and Gods. Every authentic white initiation begins here." - Samael Aun Weor, *The Aquarian Message*

Nirvana: (Sanskrit निर्वाण, "extinction" or "cessation"; Tibetan: nyangde, literally "the state beyond sorrow") In general use, the word nirvana refers to the permanent cessation of suffering and its causes, and therefore refers to a state of consciousness rather than a place. Yet, the term can also apply to heavenly realms, whose vibration is related to the cessation of suffering. In other words, if your mind-stream has liberated itself from the causes of suffering, it will naturally vibrate at the level of Nirvana (heaven).

"When the Soul fuses with the Inner Master, then it becomes free from Nature and enters into the supreme happiness of absolute existence. This state of happiness is called Nirvana. Nirvana can be attained through millions of births and deaths, but it can also be attained by means of a shorter path; this is the path of "initiation." The Initiate can reach Nirvana in one single life if he so wants it." - Samael Aun Weor, *The Zodiacal Course*

"Nirvana is a region of Nature where the ineffable happiness of the fire reigns. The Nirvanic plane has seven sub-planes. A resplendent hall exists in each one of these seven sub-planes of Nirvanic matter where the Nirmanakayas study their mysteries. This is why they call their sub-planes "halls" and not merely "sub-planes" as the Theosophists do. The Nirvanis say: "We are in the first hall of Nirvana or in the second hall of Nirvana, or in the third, or in the fourth, or fifth, or sixth, or in the seventh hall of Nirvana." To describe the ineffable joy of Nirvana is impossible. There, the music of the spheres reigns and the soul is enchanted within a state of bliss, which is impossible to describe with words." - Samael Aun Weor, *The Revolution of Beelzebub*

Sahaja Maithuna: (Sanskrit) Sahaja, "natural." Maithuna, "sacramental intercourse"

Samadhi: (Sanskrit) Literally means "union" or "combination" and its Tibetan equivilent means "adhering to that which is profound and definitive," or ting nge dzin, meaning "To hold unwaveringly, so there is no movement." Related terms include satori, ecstasy, manteia, etc. Samadhi is a state of consciousness. In the west, the term is used to describe an ecstatic state of consciousness in which the Essence escapes the painful limitations of the mind (the "I") and therefore experiences what is real: the Being, the Great Reality. There are many levels of Samadhi. In the sutras and tantras the term Samadhi has a much broader application whose precise interpretation depends upon which school and teaching is using it.

"Ecstasy is not a nebulous state, but a transcendental state of wonderment, which is associated with perfect mental clarity." - Samael Aun Weor, *The Elimination of Satan's Tail*

Semen: In the esoteric tradition of pure sexuality, the word semen refers to the sexual energy of the organism, whether male or female. This is because male and female both carry the "seed" within: in order to create, the two "seeds" must be combined. In common usage: "The smaller, usually motile male reproductive cell of most organisms that reproduce sexually." English semen originally meant 'seed of male animals' in the 14th century, and it was not applied to human males until the 18th century. It came from Latin semen, "seed of plants," from serere ˋto sow.' The Latin goes back to the Indo-European root *se-, source of seed, disseminate, season, seminar, and seminal. The word seminary (used for religious schools) is derived from semen and originally meant 'seedbed.' That the semen is the source of all virtue is known from the word "seminal," derived from the Latin "semen," and which is defined as "highly original and influencing the development of future events: a seminal artist; seminal ideas."

"According to Yogic science, semen exists in a subtle form throughout the whole body. It is found in a subtle state in all the cells of the body. It is withdrawn and elaborated into a gross form in the sexual organ under the influence of the sexual will and sexual excitement. An Oordhvareta Yogi (one who has stored up the seminal energy in the brain after sublimating the same into spiritual energy) not only converts the semen into Ojas, but checks through his Yogic power, through purity in thought, word and deed, the very formation of semen by the secretory cells or testes or seeds. This is a great secret." - Sri Swami Sivananda, *Brahmacharya* (Celibacy)

Sexual Magic: The word magic is derived from the ancient word magos "one of the members of the learned and priestly class," from O.Pers. magush, possibly from PIE *magh- "to be able, to have power." [Quoted from Online Etymology Dictionary].

"All of us possess some electrical and magnetic forces within, and, just like a magnet, we exert a force of attraction and repulsion... Between lovers that magnetic force is particularly powerful and its action has a far-reaching effect." - Samael Aun Weor, *The Mystery of the Golden Blossom*

Sexual magic refers to an ancient science that has been known and protected by the purest, most spiritually advanced human beings, whose purpose and goal is the harnessing and perfection of our sexual forces. A more accurate translation of sexual magic would be "sexual priesthood." In ancient times, the priest was always accompanied by a priestess, for they represent the divine forces at the base of all creation: the masculine and feminine, the Yab-Yum, Ying-Yang, Father-Mother: the Elohim. Unfortunately, the term "sexual magic" has been grossly misinterpreted by mistaken persons such as Aleister Crowley, who advocated a host of degenerated practices, all of which belong solely to the lowest and most perverse mentality and lead only to the enslavement of the consciousness, the worship of lust and desire, and the decay of humanity. True, upright, heavenly sexual magic is the natural harnessing of our latent forces, making them active and harmonious with nature and the divine, and which leads to the perfection of the human being.

"People are filled with horror when they hear about sexual magic; however, they are not filled with horror when they give themselves to all kinds of sexual perversion and to all kinds of carnal passion." - Samael Aun Weor, *The Perfect Matrimony*

Solar Bodies: The physical, vital, astral, mental, and causal bodies that are created through the beginning stages of Alchemy/Tantra and that provide a basis for existence in their corresponding levels of nature, just as the physical body does in the physical world. These bodies or vehicles are superior due to being created out of Solar (Christic) Energy, as opposed to the inferior, lunar bodies we receive from nature. Also known as the Wedding Garment (Christianity), the Merkabah (Kabbalah), To Soma Heliakon (Greek), and Sahu (Egyptian).

"All the Masters of the White Lodge, the Angels, Archangels, Thrones, Seraphim, Virtues, etc., etc., etc. are garbed with the Solar Bodies. Only those who have Solar Bodies have the Being incarnated. Only someone who possesses the Being is an authentic Human Being." - Samael Aun Weor, *The Esoteric Treatise of Hermetic Astrology*

White Brotherhood or Lodge: That ancient collection of pure souls who maintain the highest and most sacred of sciences: White Magic or White Tantra. It is called White due to its purity and cleanliness. This "Brotherhood" or "Lodge" includes human beings of the highest order from every race, culture, creed and religion, and of both sexes.

Index

Consciousness, 19, 36, 38, 46, 63,
70-71, 84-85, 91, 101, 103-
104, 110, 126, 138, 162, 179,
194-197, 199-201, 204-207,
212-213, 216-219
Constellations, 118
Contemplates, 27, 105
Contemplation, 91, 111, 203, 216
Control, 17-19, 49, 83, 87, 99, 105,
107, 110, 114, 137, 162, 170-
171, 181, 194, 214-215
Cord, 134, 137-138, 155-156, 161,
173, 214
Cords, 133, 155
Coronation, 36, 131
Corpse, 137
Cosmic Chrestos, 74
Cosmic Christ, 27, 74, 87
Cosmic Day, 159
Cosmic Night, 70, 83, 159
Cosmocreators, 140
Cosmos, 84, 159, 204-206
Cranium, 35, 139
Create, 77, 107, 118-119, 203, 209,
218
Created, 18, 51-53, 56, 73, 107, 170,
200, 202, 206, 219
Creating, 77, 108, 129
Creation, 2, 25, 51-52, 57, 60, 82, 85,
216, 219
Creative, 36, 57, 89, 119, 169-171,
173, 175, 199
Creator, 53, 112, 208, 211
Creators, 108, 129
Credit, 80
Creed, 175-176
Crime, 47, 113, 177, 190
Crocodile, 75-76
Cross, 29-30, 115-116, 121, 186
Crown, 13, 26, 30, 105, 115, 131,
136, 138, 171-172, 202, 204-
205, 213
Crown Chakra, 131, 138
Crown of Life, 131
Crown of Thorns, 171-172
Crucified, 63, 97, 129, 189
Crucify, 115-116

Cry, 43, 183, 187
Cult, 126-127
Cultivate, 6, 15, 66, 105-106, 111-
112, 114, 122, 211
Culture, 38, 113, 120, 206, 210
Cunning, 110
Cup, 20, 147
Cupola, 181
Cups, 147
Currents, 60, 84, 154-155, 161
Cycle, 190
Cycles, 83
Daily, 28, 52, 64, 74, 79, 106, 111,
171, 204
Damage, 108, 111, 190, 196
Damascus, 113
Dance, 186, 192
Danger, 25, 38, 99, 155, 167
Dangma, 101, 192
Daniel, 144, 193, 195-196
Darkness, 9, 15, 21, 40-42, 55, 80-81,
119-121, 152, 184
Daughter, 204
David, 205
Dawn, 24, 52, 76, 90, 129, 141, 189
Dawn of Life, 52, 76, 90, 129, 189
Dawning, 49, 211
Dead, 9, 69, 75
Death, 27, 68, 78-79, 86, 91, 105,
116, 122, 125-127, 149, 158,
160, 196, 202, 205, 208, 212,
215
Deaths, 77, 80, 140-141, 164, 175,
218
Debts, 80, 124, 140, 158, 165
Deeds, 16, 37, 80, 120, 124-125, 127,
158, 165
Defect, 104, 208, 216
Defects, 49, 104, 185
Degenerated, 93, 219
Degree, 21, 26, 35, 123, 131, 203,
206-207
Degrees, 26, 34, 36-37, 132, 138, 140,
144, 151
Demon, 113, 156, 207
Demonic, 18, 126, 156

Demons, 10, 99, 129, 157, 162, 184, 191, 207
Descartes, 70, 97
Descend, 72, 161, 181, 207, 217
Descended, 129, 158
Descending, 181, 214
Descends, 35-36, 72, 156, 161
Descent, 33
Desert, 160, 175
Desire, 10, 19, 24, 48, 74, 98-99, 119, 160, 207, 215, 219
Desired, 42, 47, 61, 68
Desires, 111, 163, 200, 207, 211, 215
Destroy, 111, 190-191, 196, 203
Devas, 31, 51-52, 62, 69, 83-85, 208
Devic, 51-53, 207
Devil, 129, 142, 175
Devolution, 2
Devotees, 62, 67, 78, 110, 116, 118, 125, 128, 137, 148, 152, 193
Devotion, 67
Dharana, 106
Dharma, 203
Dharmakaya, 70
Dhyana, 106, 202
Dhyani Buddhas, 70-71
Dhyanis, 84
Diamond, 2, 10, 91, 131, 138
Diamond Eye, 131, 138
Diamond Soul, 91
Dignity, 61, 87, 217
Direct, 31, 48, 52-53, 78, 81, 84, 96, 107, 111, 136, 193, 201, 204
Discernment, 48, 111
Discipline, 101, 103, 105, 107, 109, 111, 113, 206
Disciplines, 106, 109, 114, 206
Disequilibrium, 110, 124
Disintegrated, 126, 140-141, 164
Dislikes, 17-18
Disobedience, 40, 183
Disobeyed, 40, 93, 149
Dispel, 15
Divine Mother, 183, 208, 211, 213
Divine Soul, 36, 141
Diviners, 143-145
Divorce, 47, 156

Dog, 113, 130, 201
Dogmas, 38
Donkey, 27, 98-99
Doors, 7, 9, 23-24, 28, 31-32, 34, 67, 75, 78, 112, 148-149, 155, 164, 191
Doorway, 45
Dorsal, 75
Double, 91
Doubt, 175, 203, 208
Dove, 14, 60, 90, 152, 186, 211
Dragon, 57, 158
Drama, 64-65, 87
Dream, 103, 143-144, 170, 193-195, 200, 206
Dreams, 79, 103-104, 143-145, 193, 195-197, 207
Drink, 6, 115, 174
Drunk, 128-129
Dual, 25
Dust, 5, 44, 162
Duties, 190, 197
Duty, 180
Dynasties, 160
Eagle, 11, 159, 170
Ear, 11, 135, 138, 160
Ears, 99, 142, 181, 186
Earth, 1, 3, 6, 14, 23, 47-48, 51, 53, 56, 61-62, 72-73, 75-76, 84-85, 91, 97, 118, 123, 129-131, 133, 147-148, 158, 208-209, 211-212
Earthquakes, 82, 169
East, 52, 75, 91, 102, 133, 147, 199
Ebnico Abnicar On, 25
Economy, 62
Ecstasy, 2, 66, 101, 106, 216, 218
Effort, 1, 9, 85, 185
Egg, 27, 89, 139-140
Ego, 48, 61, 164, 194, 200-201, 203, 206-209, 211, 217
Egypt, 3, 160, 199, 208
Egyptian, 66, 75, 109, 204, 216, 219
Egyptians, 78
Eight, 79, 136
Eighteen, 78, 128-129, 147
Eighth, 158, 185, 187

Transcendental, 110, 165, 177, 203, 208, 218
Transform, 84, 88, 95, 113, 139, 180, 210, 216
Transformation, 113, 157, 205
Transmutation, 21, 88, 96, 191
Transmute, 24, 87, 117, 128, 191, 199
Transmuted, 27, 89-90, 160, 192
Treason, 114
Treatise, 68, 72, 87, 207-208, 212, 217
Treatise of Esoteric Medicine, 68, 72
Treatise of Sexual Alchemy, 87
Tree, 1, 5-6, 8, 23-26, 31, 34-35, 39, 45, 50, 57-61, 66, 68, 70-71, 79-80, 86-87, 89, 91-94, 122, 126, 140-142, 147, 149, 171, 179, 188, 216-217
Tree of Life, 8, 60, 71, 122, 140-142, 147, 216-217
Triad, 76, 90-91, 93, 126, 137, 140-141, 152, 156-157, 162, 164-166, 192, 217
Triangle, 68, 166
Triangular, 26
Tribulation, 125, 127
Tridandins, 133
Trillions, 127, 216-217
Trinity, 80, 88, 210, 214
Triveni, 133-134, 138
Truth, 48, 55, 78, 111, 138, 201, 204
Tubes, 81, 136
Tunic, 13, 15, 30-31, 39, 45, 62, 65-68, 93, 131, 160, 192
Turiya, 165, 206, 216
Turkish, 75
Twelve, 43, 53, 118, 134
Twentieth, 161
Twenty, 79
Twin, 141
Two, 20-21, 27, 29, 35-36, 42-43, 60, 77, 79, 83, 97, 103-104, 107, 123-124, 131, 133, 136, 141, 155, 173, 177, 183, 193, 197, 200, 202-204, 206-207, 209, 212, 214-215, 218

Tyr, 80
Umbilical, 156
Unconscious, 29, 107, 207
Understand, 13, 15, 39, 46, 52, 62, 70, 84, 93, 102-103, 105, 118, 139, 181, 187, 196, 199, 206-207, 213
Understanding, 179, 181, 215
Understood, 26, 42, 60, 170, 177, 187, 203, 211, 215
Union, 23, 84, 86, 119, 121, 166, 173-174, 197, 213, 218
Unite, 96, 136, 140, 152, 163
United, 60, 84-85, 103-104, 131, 152, 163-166, 171, 177, 186, 214
Unites, 36, 128, 131, 152, 205
Uniting, 136, 152
Unity, 188, 216-217
Universal Fire, 19, 23-24, 31, 70, 145, 159
Universal White Fraternity, 28, 36, 112, 158, 175-176
Urania, 161-162
Uterus, 23, 86-87, 136, 170, 173
Vago O A Ego, 61
Vain, 38, 143-145, 148, 180
Valley, 147
Vanity, 143, 149, 164
Vasomotor, 194
Vayu Tattva, 72
Vedas, 70-72, 215
Vegetable, 14, 66, 69-70, 72, 85
Vehicle, 27, 67, 87, 91, 99, 205, 216
Vehicles, 36, 69, 101-103, 118, 140, 165, 179, 219
Veins, 83, 90
Veneration, 67, 112
Ventricle, 136
Venus, 64-65, 85
Verb, 46, 49, 205, 209, 214
Vertebra, 14, 33, 123, 132-133, 135, 161, 173, 214
Vertical, 160
Vestments, 15
Vesture, 6, 13, 29, 186
Vigil, 79, 170, 194-195
Vigilance, 157, 167

Glorian Publishing is a non-profit publisher dedicated to spreading the sacred universal doctrine to suffering humanity. All of our works are made possible by the kindness and generosity of sponsors. If you would like to make a tax-deductible donation, you may send it to the address below, or visit our website for other alternatives. If you would like to sponsor the publication of a book, please contact us at (844) 945-6742 or help@ gnosticteachings.org.

Glorian Publishing
PO Box 110225
Brooklyn, NY 11211 US
Phone: (844) 945-6742

VISIT US ONLINE AT:

gnosticteachings.org